Growing Up In a Zoo

My life in St. Joseph, Mo. in the 1940's to the 1960's

By:

Larry Flinchpaugh

Front cover photo: Author, LarryFlinchpugh holding his pet
monkey, "Topper" in the Apple Blossom parade c.1948

Growing Up
In a Zoo

Personal experiences of Larry Flinchpaugh growing up
and working in his parent's zoo in St. Joseph, Missouri in
the 1940's to the 1960's

By:
Larry Flinchpaugh
St. Joseph, Missouri

Published by;
J L Flinchpaugh Publishing Company
5500 Cape Court
St. Joseph, Mo. 64503

ISBN-10 0615452078
ISBN-43 9780615452074

Third printing
January, 2012

lflinch@stjoelive.com
www.larryflinchpaugh.com

"My goal in life is to become the person my dog thinks I am"
(Author unknown)

iii

The Flinchpaugh Family
1957

Johnny

Margery

Larry

Jean

Vicky

Table of Contents

--Forward--

What was St. Joseph like 78 years before our story begins?

Early Day St. Joseph
From
The Illustrated London News, October 12, 1861

St. Joseph or St. Joe as it is irreverently called by the Americans is a pretty good town situated on the east bank of the Missouri River. It is the western terminus of the Hannibal and St. Joe Railway which completes the American system of railways westward.

St. Joe has much the same relation to the Great Plains that a seaport has to the ocean. It is the point of arrival and departure after a three month's voyage overland of hundreds of travelers and wagon trains who make the passage between California, Oregon, and the western states of the union. The passage across the mountains and over the plains is as lonely as a voyage across the ocean. Neither towns nor villages are met with, and the emigrant train has to depend upon its own resources as much as a ship does while navigating the sea.

There is a wild look about the people of St. Joe. Nearly everybody carries a rifle and has that peculiar expression of countenance which indicates the possession of the ability to take care of himself and cut up particularly rough if interfered with. Some awful roughs may be seen about occasionally but these are held in good check by the respectable portion of the place; and although St. Joe is a wild, out-of-the-way place, almost beyond the reach of the law, yet the people go about as safely and carry on their business as securely, as if they were in the neighborhood of Boston. Should any of the border ruffian class attempt any villainy, lynch law would most likely cut short his career and he might find himself hanging to the branch of a tree before he had time to engage council to prove his innocence of the crime which he was caught in the act of executing. It is an event and a picturesque scene to see one of **the long trains of wagons arrive from the westward**, the people looking so brown and weatherworn and the children healthy and happy, and the rush all make immediately on certain shops and stores. One great delight on the party of the men seems to be to get themselves shaved as clean as possible. Fine bright colored shirts and handkerchiefs are immediately obtained and ostentatiously exhibited.

Market day at St. Joe is a peculiar sight and gives one a better idea of the back-settlement life than can be obtained anywhere else. The farmer and his family, in their particular wagon, which with the exception of the wheels they have made themselves are things to be seen. There is no place in the United States where greater variety of character, interesting incidents, and opportunity for the study of the human nature exists to a greater extent than at St. Joe on the Missouri.

Preface

It has often been said that there is at least one book within each and every one of us. Now that I have just celebrated my 71st birthday, I tend to agree. Earlier in my life, before retiring, I was so busy making a living and providing for my family, I had little time or even the inclination to write a book. As you get older you begin to reminisce about the good old days and enjoy sharing your memories with others.

I have had many friends and acquaintances tell me that I should write a book about my experiences in growing up with such a wide array of unusual animals. Hopefully some of my experiences will be entertaining and maybe some will even evoke a few laughs. Additionally I will describe for you my memories of what life was like in the 1940's and 50's in St. Joseph, Missouri for a kid growing up with just about every animal imaginable for a pet.

I am sure that there are many people from St. Joe and the surrounding areas that have fond memories of visiting my parent's animal businesses, starting with the Pet Shop on South 8th Street and then on 12th and Frederick Avenue, to the Reptile Garden and Zoo on Frederick Avenue just east of the Belt Highway.

My father, Johnny Flinchpaugh, had worked for the Loose Wiles Biscuit Company as a traveling salesman but in 1932 he quit his salesman job to pursue his passion for animals. He opened the **"Plainview Wild Animal Farm** and **"Silver Fox Service Station"** near Kirksville, Missouri. In addition to having animals on display and charging admission to view them, he supplied animals to various circuses.

He opened a pet shop in St. Joe at 603 South Eighth Street (8th and Messanie) in 1946 and in 1951 he moved it to 1202 Frederick Avenue. (Northeast of the City Hall) In 1953 he moved the Pet Shop to 3727 Frederick (now the location of the Citizens Bank and Trust Company). At this larger location it was called, "Flinchpaughs Pet Shop, Reptile Gardens and Zoo" and sometimes "The Monkey Jungle." The story you are about to read involves my life of literally growing up in a zoo and exploring the many changes from the 1940's to the present in St. Joseph, Missouri.

In 1963 my father sold his Zoo property in St. Joe and moved to Muscatine, Iowa to become the Director of the Weed Park Zoo. In 1975 he and my mother Margery returned to St. Joseph to retire. My mother passed away March 16, 1985 at age 77 and my father on January 21, 1989 at the age of 82.

This is actually the fourth book that I have published. The first book was **"The Flinchpaugh Family History and Genealogy** (a copy is at the Genealogy Library in downtown St. Joseph). My 2nd book, **"Secrets of Our Hidden Controllers Revealed"** was published in December, 2009 and my third book (pamphlet) is a reprint with my comments that was originally published by Pastor Sheldon Emry entitled **"Billion$ For the Banker$- Debts for the People."** *I recommend that you read both my "Secrets..." book and the **"Billion$ For the Banker$..."** pamphlet if you are sincerely interested in taking part in returning our country to that which was envisioned by our founding fathers.*

Chapter One

In the Beginning...

On April 16, 1939, Joseph Stalin had requested a British, French and Russian anti-Nazi pact. That was the same day I was born in St. Joseph, Missouri at the Missouri Methodist Hospital. My full name is John Larry Flinchpaugh but I have always gone by "Larry"—probably to differentiate me from my father whose first name was also John.

I have pictures of when my family lived on Corby Street but since I was only an infant my earliest memories are of living at 2614 Duncan Street. Hall School, where I would later attend Kindergarten through Sixth grade, was at the top of the hill.

Bauman's Grocery Store was just around the corner on 27th street where I learned to gamble at an early age. We neighborhood kids inserted pennies into the gum ball machine in an attempt to get the yellow ball with red stripes. If we were lucky and got the yellow ball, it could be traded for a 5 cent candy bar. When we didn't have any pennies, we would gather up a few pop bottles and sell them to the store for 2 cents each. Millard Fisher's Grocery Store was about a block further towards Mitchell Ave. (Dr Yurth's chiropractic office is there today). Mr. Dearing's Barber Shop and Jerre Anne's Cafeteria were near 27th and Mitchell with a Standard Oil Service station across the street where we would have our bicycle tires repaired.

It seemed as if almost everything was within walking distance in those days. That is probably because we, like most people, had only one car and we had to do much walking; dad always drove our car to work.

Television didn't really get popular until about 1953 so going to the movie theater was a great treat. We could walk to The Plaza Theater at 1830 Olive and The Hickory Theater that was a little farther at 2235 South 11th, or we could ride the bus if we wanted to go to the other theatres. The Missouri, Electric, and Orpheum Theatres were on Edmond Street in downtown St. Joe and The Jo was nearby at 124 North 3rd street. The Uptown Theatre was at 21st and Frederick which is now occupied by The Lehr Construction Company. Wades Indian Grill was directly across the street from The Uptown before it moved over to Mitchell Avenue. The Rialto and The King were in South St. Joe and The Regal was on St. Joseph Avenue.

Later when I was a teenager we had the drive in theatres like The Skylark at 137 North Belt (now Hy-Vee) which was opened in about 1948 and just a year before, The Belt Drive In where Oakland Avenue meets the Belt Highway. The Cow Town Theatre was in South St. Joe on Lake Contrary road.

The Drive In movie concept was invented and patented by Richard M. Hollingshead Jr. in 1933. His idea was to offer conveniences that the regular theatres couldn't provide. When we went to the drive in, our parents didn't need to hire a baby sitter, we didn't need to get dressed up, parking was included in the price of admission, and it was a great place to take a date for dinner and a movie under the stars.

It was sheer magic going to the drive in theatres. I can remember the long line of cars along the shoulder on the belt highway waiting to get tickets. Some people even put two or three people in the trunk so as to get them in for free. Of course, I only heard of other people doing this but never tried it myself. As you went in there was an usher with a flashlight motioning to you where there was an empty place to park. As soon as we got parked, the young children would run up to the play ground under the screen and play until the movie started. You could hear the sound of the gravel crunching under the tires and could hardly breathe from the huge cloud of dust from the 200-300 cars maneuvering for a choice place to park. During the intermission, between the double feature, everyone ran for the concession stand and bathroom. It was so exciting to bring back a cardboard tray with popcorn, soda pop, hot dogs and candy and watch the movie on the huge outdoor screen. In the early days the movies were usually the Grade B variety because the large movie producers who owned many of the brick and mortar theatres saw the Drive In's as competitors so refused to rent them the first run movies. This later changed but was a real problem in the beginning years of the drive Ins.

Even though I don't remember this happening in St. Joe, but in other cities the Drive In Theaters owners, in order to get more customers, offered other service like buying your groceries for you while you watched the movie or would wash your clothes in their own laundry facilities. I heard that some would even change flat tires and change the oil in your car.

As a teenager, I used to go to Ben Magoons on South Eight Street and buy pastrami sandwiches on pumpernickel bread and potato salad and pick up a carton of beer and take my date to one of the drive Ins. I usually picked out a movie I had already seen so I wouldn't need to be bothered with watching it.

By the 1970's and 80's most Drive Ins were sold to developers for shopping centers or housing projects. It was a wonderful experience while it lasted.

My wife, Phyllis Nelson who grew up in South Park, remembers attending at least one movie shown outside behind the old Picket School on Picket Road a short distance east of the Belt Highway. Folks took blankets to sit on the ground and hoped they wouldn't get eaten up by the mosquitoes. The movie she remembers was "Our Town" which had something to do with Heaven. Coincidently that is the same name (with St. Joe added) of the 1950's promotional film that I show at the city libraries and at local civic groups. She remembers hearing of some of the small towns around St. Joe that also showed movies on Friday or Saturday night, in the city parks.

The movies, or the "Picture Show", as we called them, usually had the feature movie and a short like Candid Camera, the Pathe News Reel and a cartoon. Sometimes there was a musical short with a bouncing ball dancing over the lyrics that were written at the bottom of the screen. The audience was supposed to sing along with the movie sound track. Often a double feature was offered.

The kids' movies that I attended on Saturday were usually at the Plaza Theatre located at 1830 Olive or the Electric Theatre at 708 Edmond (Across the street from the Missouri Theater). Kid's tickets were only 15 cents, but some Saturday mornings you could get in for free for the special shows if you had 15 Pepsi Cola bottle caps.

My favorite movies at that time were the Westerns featuring Roy Rogers, Gene Autry, Johnny Mack Brown, or Lash Larue. One time Gene Autry actually appeared in person at the Electric Theatre. Almost all of the westerns ended the same way; the hero never married the heroine and at the end of the movie would slowly ride off into the sunset while the beautiful girl and her father were waving to him. The directors of these movies didn't seem to have any imagination-they all ended the same way. Other favorites of mine were Abbot and Costello, The Three Stooges, Laurel and Hardy and the Bowery Boys featuring Leo Gorcey and Huntz Hall.

A sad memory for me was that Blacks, prior to about 1954, were only allowed to go to the Orpheum Theatre and there they had to sit in the balcony. I remember thinking that this wasn't right but at such a young age I just had to accept it. As I got a little older I began to voice my opinion on this issue and consequently upset some of my friends and family members who didn't agree with me. As it turned out, I would continue this practice of voicing my opinion on such controversial subjects such as discrimination, politics, and religion throughout my adult life.

 In the early 1960's while one of my relatives and myself were watching TV, he sarcastically made the remark about a famous black singer, "Leslie Uggams must think she is as good as us." I was shocked at this statement and quickly commented that none in our family could sing, she probably had more money than all of us put together and she was much prettier than anyone in our family. My comments didn't go over very well at the time but I felt good about expressing myself and showing how wrong he was in thinking Negroes were inferior to Whites. Fortunately, as the years went by and like most whites began to have more contact with blacks, his opinion changed.

What really bothered me was that many people who degraded the Negro race in the 1950's professed to be "good Christians." I thought, something is seriously wrong here. How could anyone with such high Christian ideals feel this way about Blacks? Do they think Blacks have a different God from Whites? This could be one of the reasons why, later in life, I have been so critical of religion. In my opinion the "Christians" should have been able to solve the integration problem without any help from the government. Sadly, nearly 100 years of suffering after the great Civil War passed before much improvement was seen. (1865-1965)

It seemed like every neighborhood had a bar or several bars to entertain the men getting off work from Goetz Brewery, Western Tablet Factory, Armour's and Swifts. The TV series "Cheers" reminded me a lot of the St Joe bars; a good place to have a cold beer and meet all your old friends. The first evening after turning 21, I went to the New Yorker on Frederick Avenue which was owned by my good friend, Fred Chitwood's parents, and "Turas 420 Club", on South 6th Street as I recall. Once, before I had turned 21, I was in a bar with my cousin and picked up an empty bottle of beer from a couple's table that was leaving. I set the empty bottle on the bar and said to the bartender, "I would like another bottle of Bud." It worked, the bartender must have thought he had already checked my ID. I thought I was pretty clever. Strangely enough, I seldom drink today.

It is depressing to think of all the businesses that were here during my childhood that are mere memories today. I remember the delicious smells of the bakeries as we drove near Penn and 11th Streets and along Frederick Avenue at 24th, the Wonder Bakery and the Rainbow Bakery. When one would go to the corner grocery he would usually push the door open with a bar advertising one of these bakeries.

Speaking of the corner grocery store brings back many nostalgic memories. Many people did their shopping, or as they called it their "trading" at the corner grocery while others often made a weekly trek to a supermarket such as one of the Safeways, Greenhills, or A&Ps. The corner grocery was a marvelous place for the kids to head for when they had a few pennies to spend. The array of penny candy was a delight to see, and if we had a whole nickel to spend wow, we could get a nice sized candy bar or even a bottle of pop or an ice cream bar! Those grocers must have been saints to be able to wait until the kid made his final decision.

A few years later when the price of candy had gone up considerably, I asked the clerk how much a snicker was. He said they were two for a quarter. I then told him that I only wanted one and he said that it would be 15 cents. I told him that I would take the other one. This story reminded me of an incident a friend of mine had in Bakersfield, California a few years ago. She went to a bicycle shop to purchase a bike for one of her sons. The clerk said, "This is your lucky day, the bikes are 10% off." She said, maybe I should get another one for my other son." The clerk then said "you would then save 20%." She thought a minute and said, "I think I will buy 10 bikes." The clerk still didn't understand that using this type of reasoning, 10 bikes would be free.

Moms didn't always have as much sandwich makings on hand as moms of today in their large refrigerators, so when we woke up to rain we often were sent to the corner grocery for lunch meat and bread so that we would be able to take our lunch to school rather than walking home in the rain for lunch. I remember often going to the meat counter and asking for a dime's worth of minced ham. I remember my mother wrapping my lunch in a newspaper and tied with a string because we didn't have a paper sack.

Many people didn't have a car, and those who did usually had only one. My mother and I used to ride the bus to go downtown to shop. Almost always there would be a stop at one of the Dime Stores, Kresges, Woolworths or Mattinglys.

I can still smell the perfumes and powders in the ladies' sections in the large department stores. I liked to go to the mezzanine and look out over the balcony to the first floor. There was usually a Black woman operating the elevator in the larger stores. A few years later when the elevators became automated many people were afraid to ride without a human at the controls. I'm sure they thought "What would I do if the doors failed to open!"

Usually the first thing I would do after arriving at Hirsch's at Eighth and Felix Streets was to head to the basement to the toy department. I especially liked to buy the red rubber molds and plaster to cast my own figurines, my "works of art". The first ones I bought were a turkey, an owl, and an Indian Chief bust. They were a lot of fun to make and then paint.

The sidewalks would be full of busy shoppers dressed in their Sunday best. There were many very nice men's clothiers such as Plymouth. And for women, as per my wife, there were The Paris, Mode O Day, The Holly Shop and many more. When one needed jewelry Joe Opticians always came to mind although there were many other jewelry stores as well. During the holidays or for a special treat there was the beautiful little Russell Stover's candy store. Of course one could purchase most of one's candy needs at Kresge's and probably at Woolworth's and Mattinglys too. I remember Grants had a pretty nifty candy and cookie counter also. My favorite was the hot nuts in the waxed bag. If we were still shopping during lunch time we would usually eat at the Kresge's lunch counter or at the Oakford Tea Room on North 7th near the Mannschreck's Book Store. Later on during the 50s we sometimes frequented the Maid Rite sandwich shop on Edmond at 7th.

Downtown, or as some would say, Uptown, was full of offices including most all doctors' offices. But if you were unable to get to the doctor's office he would usually go to your home. This was very convenient for the mother of several sick children or one with no means of transportation except the bus. I think the home visits usually occurred at the end of the day.

The Apple Blossom Parade, winding through downtown was a sight to see on a Friday afternoon in May. The children, dismissed from school, lined the curbs, the adults standing many deep to get a look. The Parade was so grand, dozens of surrounding towns sent their school marching bands to join our local ones. People came from miles around. Many stayed for the carnival that evening which was set up in or near the park surrounding the City Hall.

The next day after the big parade there was a children's parade where costumed children would march and show off their pets and decorated trikes, bikes, etc. What fun!

Another memory of downtown was the March of Dimes celebration. I don't know where the line started or ended but I remember the line of dimes stretching along Felix Street.

There is so much more that could be written about Downtown but to do so would take a book in itself. Downtown was truly the center of our city, the memories of what was and what is now almost make me cry. I have often thought how fortunate we have been that the city fathers did not move the Court House to the Belt Highway. I made the comment to Marshall White a couple of years ago that it is a good thing that the Roman Coliseum was not built in St. Joe, because there would probably be a Wal Mart or parking garage there today. The next morning my comments were in the St. Joseph News Press.

My earliest memory of my dad's work was with Loose Wiles Biscuit Company. Dad was a traveling salesman selling cookies and crackers all over Northwest Missouri. He would often bring home cookie display samples in black boxes with cellophane over them for the kids to play with. We couldn't eat them but sure had fun playing "store" with them. Sometimes he would bring me the life sized cut outs of human figures advertising some product and I would set them up all over the house and pretend they were real people. My wife remembers her dad bringing home a cardboard standing man when she was about three and placing him in their bathroom which enabled her to go there without having to have someone take her. "Joe" was her protector.

Every spring a man would come down our alley on Duncan Street with a horse and plow and for about a dollar would plow up a lot behind our house for a garden. I remember our garden and house as being huge. A few years ago I went back to visit my house on Duncan street and could hardly believe how small it was. I guess when you are only three or four feet tall you see things from a different perspective. All kinds of memories came rushing back to me. I can actually remember holding on to the bars of my baby bed while at the same time jumping up and down to cause the bed to move out of the bedroom into the hallway enabling me to see what was going on in the living room.

There is a "Time Capsule" under the front porch inside the brick post on the west side of the house. About 1949 I lowered a jar into the hollow brick post that contained some pennies and a note describing my secret code that my friends and I were using. The rope slipped out of my hands and the jar has remained in the hollow post every since. I have often thought of asking the present owners of the house to allow me to retrieve the time capsule.

Winters were especially fun in St. Joe! It seemed that it always snowed at Christmas time. On Christmas morning I could actually see Santa's sleigh tracks in the snow. What an imagination! When there was a full moon and the ground was covered with snow, it was sometimes light enough, even at midnight, to read a newspaper outside.

The kids in the neighborhood would take their sleds to the top of the hill near Hall school, run and take a flying leap on them and go for a whole block before stopping. One person always volunteered to watch for cars at the bottom of 26th street. If you didn't have a sled, the grocery store would provide you with a huge rainbo bread cardboard box that when unfolded made a great toboggan. All you had to do was unfold it and sit on top holding on to the flaps while someone gave you a starting push down the snow covered hill. Many times I would stay outside in the cold too long which caused my hands and feet to be itching so badly that I had to soak them in cold water to warm them up gradually.

Many of my toys were home made. I don't think we were poor but it just seemed more fun to make our own. One of my favorites was a soap box derby type of car. I would find an old discarded two by eight piece of wood about 4 feet long and would attach wagon wheels to both ends. The front 2x4 axel was attached to the 2 x 8 with only one large spike so that I could put my feet on it for steering. A bolt would have been much better but I probably didn't have a bolt. As far as that goes I also didn't have a drill to drill a hole for it either. Unlike today, not everyone had an electric drill. The front of the car usually had half of a wooden orange crate for a hood and the make believe engine compartment. I would nail 2 tin cans on the front to simulate head lights. Trying to stop this monster was a real problem. Usually I would just drag my feet, but sometimes I would nail a stick with rubber wrapped around it to the side of the 2 x 8, and when it was pulled it would drag the ground. This made a nice black mark all the way down the sidewalk and didn't really slow down the car that much.

That was almost as much fun as fastening a playing card with a spring type close pin to the bicycle spokes on the tires. It made your bike sound like an airplane. Also putting marbles in your dad's car hubcaps was fun, but I don't believe my dad felt the same way.

Another favorite toy of mine was the tin can telephone. We would punch two small holes in two cans and tie a long piece of kite string between the two. My friends and I could actually communicate several hundred feet. Also I made stilts from cans by attaching wires on each side of the can, and pulling up hard on the wires so they would stay on my feet. Also we made stilts out of scrap lumber; not as tall as the circus clowns.

Once I took a saw and cut a scrap of wood into the shape of a boat with a cut out at the back. By stretching a rubber band across the cut-out and winding a small piece of wood around it, I had a motor to propel the boat.

There was a wooded lot next to the third house up the street. It was next to Mr. Winter's house. Once we dug a hole and covered it with logs, cardboard, and dirt so that we could have a secret hideout. When someone would chase us into the woods, we would just disappear into our secret underground fort. We could hear them up above saying, "Where did they go?" Mickey Lamb, Gary Winfrey and I sure had fun building our fort but eventually my dad made us fill in the hole because he thought it was too dangerous and might collapse on us.

I used to build miniature forts from small sticks found in the yard and place dry grass around it. With a little squirt of my dad's lighter fluid the fort would really burn. You could almost hear the Indians yelling and screaming as the raging fire engulfed the fort. A few fire crackers strategically place in the fort helped make it more realistic. I can't believe I did such stupid and dangerous stunts without burning the house down. Years later I worried that my own two sons might do something like that with matches and burn our house down. So when they were around seven and eight years old I showed them how dangerous matches could be. I took them out onto our back patio in Bartlesville, Oklahoma where we lived at the time and set up two pie pans; one had dry grass in it and the other had

13

just water. We threw a lit match into each pan. The grass immediately burned and the water extinguished the match in the other pan. I explained that if the match had been dropped in our yard with the extremely dry grass that our entire house could burn down. I never told them about my childhood experience in burning make believe forts.

During World War II, I remember going to the grocery store with my mother to buy sugar and coffee and having to use war ration stamps to purchase them. These items were scarce and needed for the war effort. This was the government's way of making sure the consumer did not waste such items. Tires and gasoline were also rationed. Even in Missouri we would have air raid drills at night. All the street lights would go out and every one would darken their homes for a few minutes. I don't remember being afraid; I guess I really didn't understand what was going on. My Uncle Donald and Uncle Robert both fought in the Second World War, but being born in 1939, I don't remember much about it.

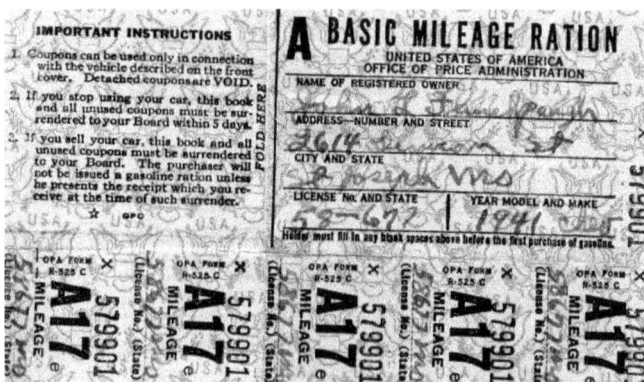

Sample war ration stamps.

I do remember my dad getting a letter from the government saying that he had to enlist for the war. My mother was very sad that he was about to be drafted. Fortunately for Mother, Jean, and I, Dad was not accepted because the next day he had a birthday and was then too old to be drafted. I think the war was over just a few months later anyway.

As I have gotten older, I have come to realize that a draft should never be needed. If our country is ever invaded, there will be plenty of volunteers to protect us. Only when we are meddling in the affairs of other countries, do we need a draft.

All kids have their favorite toys and I think most of us wish we would have kept some of them. It's a lot more expensive to buy them back years later. My favorite toys were a 16 mm movie projector, an army pup tent, a Marx train set, a Schucco toy car that had a gear shift including reverse and a steering wheel that actually worked, a battery operated telephone system, a crystal radio set, and of course every kid's favorite-the bike.

One Christmas season my mother and I were shopping at the Firestone Auto Store on 22nd near Lafayette Street when I spotted a 16mm Keystone child's movie projector. This one with an electric motor was quite an improvement over the hand cranked one I had received two years earlier. Somehow Santa Claus knew that I wanted that motorized projector because it was under the Christmas tree on Christmas morning. I still have the Keystone projector but can't remember what happened to the hand operated projector.

The first film that I purchased was "Our Gang" where the kids made their own back yard rail road powered by a dog running on a treadmill hooked to the wheels. The full length theatre version was made in 1924 and produced by

Hal Roach. It was titled; "The Sun Down Limited" My version was only about 50 feet (no sound) so lasted for about a minute. The other films I had were "Lion and Tiger Fight", "Abbot and Costello", and "Mickey Mouse". I showed the same films each week in our basement charging five cents for the movie and five cents for popcorn and Kool Aid. Nobody seemed to mind that the movies were always the same. Remember, this was before television. Once in a while I would save up enough money to buy a new movie which always packed the house that week.

One Friday night, my dad, returning from his traveling salesman job, brought me an army surplus pup tent. The first thing I did was set it up in the back yard and invited friends over to sleep outdoors. We took our flashlights and snacks out to the tent and everything was fine until it got really dark and the mosquitoes started biting. Also the cold wet dew made it extremely uncomfortable. It was about 11 pm when we all trooped inside to sleep the rest of the night. Roughing it was not as much fun as we had thought.

One Christmas I received a Marx train set- one of my favorite toys-while the rich kids got either a Lionel or American Flyer train set. Since I hadn't kept it after I grew up I had to buy one just like it at an antique show a few years ago for $100. The original in the 1940s was probably only $10 or $12. But I was lucky to find the same model as the one I had as a kid, and it even included the original box. In the 1940's the accessories were a little expensive for me so I purchased buildings, etc., that were made out of cardboard. The painted art work on the buildings made them look like real buildings. I set up my train and all it's accessories in the attic where it wouldn't be disturbed by the rest of the family.

We had a parakeet that liked to ride on the engine. He would always fly away just before the engine started to go through the tunnel. Looking back, this doesn't seem to be the way a parakeet should have been treated, but at the time I thought it was a lot of fun to see how close he would come to the tunnel before flying away.

My German Shucco toy sports car was very expensive at the time. It probably cost about $3.00 and had to be purchased from a hobby store rather than at a store like Woolworths. A really neat store was the Model Supply Shop at 905 Frederick Avenue. They sold quality model cars, planes, trains and accessories, etc. Even as a kid I recognized the high quality and craftsmanship. Today a new Shucco sells for over $80, and one from the 1940's will cost over $100 if you can find one on EBay or in an antique shop.

Santa brought me a toy telephone system one Christmas and I was able to run wires from the attic to the basement and I learned how to attach dry cell batteries to them so they would actually work. I consequently had my own personal phone in the attic, one on the main floor of the house, and one in the basement which actually worked as an intercom in our house.

Later while in Cub Scouts, I purchased a Morse Code Set and tried to learn the code. It was very difficult to learn at the time. I didn't really get proficient with it until several years later when I got my Novice Ham Radio License in about 1954. Milt Hanson of the St. Joseph ham radio club conducted a class to teach the newcomers how to send and receive Morse code. His teaching methods made it much simpler. He first taught us the letters T, M, and O which were one dash, two dashes and three dashes respectively.

Next came the letters E, I, S, H. and the number five. They were one dot, two dots, three dots, four dots, and five dots. The letter "A" was **dot dash** and the letter "N" was **dash dot**. In the first class we had learned ten characters. Also he explained a short cut that made your mind work faster by changing the words **dots and dashes** to **di for dots and dah for dashes;** which made the mental process more efficient. This simple process made it much easier to learn the code. In no time at all I was able to communicate with others like me around the world using a homemade shortwave transmitter, telegraph key and receiver.

My first transmitter was a "Philmore Kit" (three tubes) with a 5Y3 rectifier, a 6V6 oscillator and a 6L6 final amplifier. It took several weeks for me to build it because I had to learn to solder first. I quickly learned how painful it was to drop molten solder on your leg. The instructions were pretty simple, i.e.; connect wire from terminal lug F1 (S) to 5Y3 tube pin number 3 (NS). (No solder)

One of my most exciting contacts was with a DC3 mail plane. I only talked to him for about 30 minutes but in that short time he had flown through several states. He confirmed our contact by mailing me what is called a "QSL Card." One tried to get as many confirmed contacts as possible from all states, continents, and countries. The ARRL, Amateur Radio Relay League would give you an award (certificate) after successfully completing contacting each group.

This was pretty exciting for a teenager before the invention of the cell phone or as my granddaughter Emily called it at age 3, the "cellaphone." As a teenager having a radio in my dad's car that could communicate around the world was pretty neat—not even the police cars could do that. However, my dad wasn't too exited about it. The static bothered him and he was always embarrassed when the tall antenna on the back of our station wagon tore down the colored pennants strung across a service station parking lot.

Learning to ride a bike wasn't easy, but once learned I remember having such a feeling of freedom. It was easier and faster to travel several miles on a bike than by walking. My friends and I would ride out to the end of Duncan Street and continue on into the countryside to the 102 and Platte Rivers. The bridge had washed out years ago and hadn't been replaced, so we couldn't go any further. Sometimes I would go there with Dad to fish, but it was more fun to just throw rocks into the water and look for snakes and turtles.

It seems strange but I can still remember my first two phone numbers, 2-1096 and 4-2988. Our phone on Duncan Street was odd looking. It was a small black box with the dial on top and a cradle on the side for the receiver. It looked like it belonged in a grocery store. Most people, if they had a phone at all, had only one in the 1940's and 50's.

When my mother and I took the bus downtown to go shopping we would watch for the bus out our back bedroom window. When we spotted it, we ran out of the house and down to the corner to catch it. If a black woman, or a Negro woman as they were called in those days, got on the bus and there were no empty seats my mother would have me get up and give my seat to her. I have always respected black people and other minorities. I guess that is because of the way my mother and father brought me up. I feel so fortunate today for this positive attitude I have for the minority races. I have not been plagued, like many people, with the problems of segregation or integration. I am fortunate to have one daughter-in-law who is Vietnamese; another who is a Filipino, and a sister-in-law who is from Indonesia.

You don't realize until you are older how important the lessons learned from your parents are. I wish I could tell my mother and father, "Thank you for this gift". I wonder how many more of these gifts I received from them but just can't consciously remember.

One of my favorite activities when I was a kid was putting on a neighborhood circus in my back yard. We would hang two blankets on a clothes line with safety pins and open them in the center when the show was to begin. Every kid in the neighborhood would bring their dog, each dog being able to perform one trick, such as "sitting up" or "rolling over." Before long my dad was bringing home animals from our pet shop to perform in the circus, I especially remember him bringing home a monkey which really went over big with the other kids.

Television didn't become popular until after World War ll, and they were very expensive at first. We couldn't afford one in the beginning and my dad didn't want one anyway because he claimed the snowy picture gave him a headache. Before actually getting our first TV, I would sit on the floor listening to our console radio and imagine what it would be like being able to actually see who was talking. It seemed unbelievable that you could send a picture through the air.

Luckily the Stapleton's across the street, owners of Acme Radio Supply Company had an Admiral television set with a small 12 inch round picture tube. The year was about 1951. The whole neighborhood would gather at their house about four in the afternoon to watch TV as the programming started for the day. We would line up chairs in the Stapleton's dining room and turn out all the lights to make the snowy picture easier to see.

At first WDAF channel 4 in Kansas City was the only station St. Joe received. We would stare at the TV for about an hour before the programming started, watching a test pattern with round circles and a picture of an Indian. We didn't want to miss the start of the days programming. The test pattern allowed the serviceman time to adjust the pictures vertical and horizontal parts of the picture. Of course everything was black and white, so if we wanted color TV we would buy a piece of clear plastic at the dime store that had blue coloring at the top for the sky, orange in the middle for human faces and green at the bottom for grass. You just stuck it on the face of the TV screen. If you were watching a ball game it worked pretty well. Everything else looked kind of stupid. The plastic piece only cost about 10 cents. To make the picture larger in those early days of TV, there was a huge magnifying glass on a stand that could be positioned directly in front of the small screen.

The next channels that came on the air were Channel 5 KCMO, Channel 9 KMBC, both in Kansas City, and finally Channel 2 KFEQ (Now KQTV) in St. Joe. Having channels 4, 5 and 9 meant that we now had all three networks. (CBS, NBC, and ABC-in contrast to the hundreds that we now have with cable) St Joe's channel two was a network duplication but the picture was clearer than the Kansas City channel plus the news was local and some programming was different.

Before we had our own TV set, we would sit in our car outside the Midland Empire Appliance store on 12th and Frederick Avenue to watch the Ed Sullivan Show. The appliance store had installed a speaker on the outside of the store so we could hear the audio. My dad finally bought a TV, a 16 inch Raytheon in about 1953 for $250.00. You could buy a fairly nice used car in the 1950's for $250.00 to $300.00. With an antenna on the roof we could receive channels 2, St. Joseph and channels 4, 5, and 9 in Kansas City, Mo.

Trading comic books was lots of fun in the 1940s and 1950's. Three or four of us would get together and trade one for one. There was a store about three doors south of our Pet Shop on 8th street that would trade two of ours for one of his or sell you one for 5 cents. Most of the new comics cost 10 cents each. My favorites were Superman, Captain Marvel, Batman, Spider Man, Wonder Woman, Archie, Nancy and of course Donald Duck and Mickey Mouse.

When I was about ten years old my dad gave me one of his favorite childhood books called, "The Book of Woodcraft." This book was fantastic—it told how to build a tee pee, track wild animals, cook in the out of doors, identify all kinds of animals and plants, how to build a fire, Indian signs and their meanings, how to mark a trail so some one could follow you, etc. It still gets me excited just writing about it. It probably predated the boy scouts and their scouting manual.

Several years later, as an adult, I went to the library in Bartlesville, Oklahoma to look for a book on genealogy. As I was walking down this long isle toward the genealogic section, looking neither left nor right, one book came into my view, seemed to just pop off the shelf. And guess what that book was? It was my old favorite, the "Book of Woodcraft." I couldn't believe it. I wasn't even looking for that book. It gave me goose bumps all over. How could this have happened?

What I learned from this experience was that our senses are constantly recording everything around us even when we are not consciously aware of it. Have you ever been in a distant state with license plates the farthest thing from your mind, when you seem to see every car with a Missouri license plate? You are not consciously looking for Missouri license plates but they just seem to pop out of nowhere and into your mind. When your senses detect something that has meaning to you, it is immediately brought to the fore-front of you mind. Your mind is like a computer. Everything you have ever experienced is recorded and always there. You might want to consider this before allowing "trash" or negative experiences to enter.

I feel like I really had a great childhood. Not only was I able to have many enjoyable experiences with exotic animals, my parents taught me about right and wrong and stressed honesty and hard work by example.

My sister Jean, even though she used to curl my hair like a girl, was a great sister.(nine years older than I) Like any brother and sister we used to fight a little but made up easily. It only took a dime from her boy friends to get me to leave them alone and go to Herman's Drug Store on the corner of 26th and Mitchell for ice cream. One of my sister's boy friends was in the air force and took me flying in a small plane at Rosecrans Field. I thought that was pretty neat. I would later take flying lessons at Rosecrans Field when I was a student at Central High School.

The televisions shown on the next page are representative of the ones we had in the 1950's shortly after WW ll. In the 1950's I didn't think of these as TV's, rather as a radio with a picture. I have often thought that it was too bad the TV wasn't invented before the radio. Then when the radio

23

was invented, we could have had a TV that you didn't have to watch. At the time many people believed that TV would mark the end of the movie theatres.

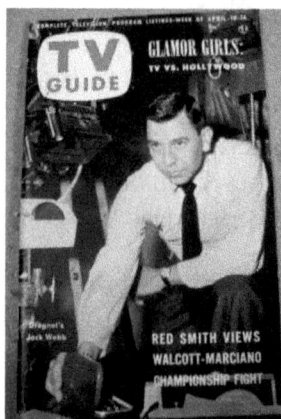

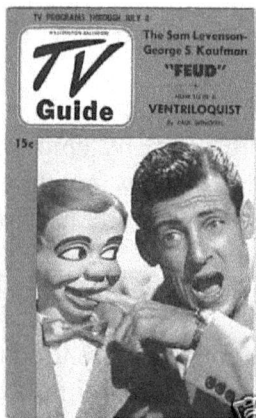

(Left) Dragnet staring Jack Webb (Right) Paul Winchell And Jerry Mahoney

Many of the first TV programs were old "B" grade movies from the 1930's or old movie serials where at the end of the program a keg of dynamite would explode next to where the hero was tied to a barrel. To find out what happened, you would have to watch this same serial the next day. When they were shown at the movie theatre, it would entice you to return to the theatre next week to see if your hero had really been killed. Of course they always survived in some miraculous way.

Radio Program Log
(1940's)

Radio Programs

Station	Kilocycles
KFEQ, St. Joseph	680
WOW, Omaha	590
KFAB, Lincoln	1110
WDAF, Kansas City	610
KMBC, Kansas City	980
WHB, Kansas City	880
KVAK, St. Joseph-Atchison	1450

THIS EVENING

5:00—KFEQ—Terry and the Pirates.
    KMBC—Texas Rangers.
5:15—WDAF—Guiding Light.
    KFEQ Music You Like.
5:30—KFEQ—Jack Armstrong.
    KMBC—Big Brother Club.
    WDAF—Fighting Leathernecks.
5:45—WHB—Tom Mix.
    KFAB—The World Today.
5:55—KFEQ—Local Brevities.
6:00—KFEQ—Musical Promenade.
    KVAK—Fulton Lewis.
    WDAF—Supper Club.
6:15—WDAF—News of the World.
    KMBC—The World Today.
6:25—KMBC—Joseph Harsch, News.
6:30—KFEQ—UP News.
    KMBC—Easy Aces.
    WOW—Jimmy Fidler.
6:40—KFEQ—Dinnertime Melodies.
6:45—WDAF—C. V. Stansell, News.
7:00—KFEQ—Top of the Evening.
    WDAF—Mr. and Mrs. North.
    KMBC, KFAB—Jack Carson.
7:15—KFEQ—Variety Show.

Kukla, Fran and Ollie

(Below) This was an early TV puppeteer show created by Burr Tillstrom. Although it started in 1947, the first NBC broadcast of the show was on January 12, 1949.

Fran Allison, a singer and radio comedian, was usually the only human to appear on screen.

Other Favorites:

Another kids' favorites was "Howdy Doody." with a frontier/western theme. It was created and produced by E. Roger Muir. and broadcast on NBC from 1947 until 1960.

Bob Smith (November 27, 1917 – July 30, 1998), the show's host, was dubbed "Buffalo Bob."Although my favorite puppet was "Howdy Doody", Mr. Fluster" and "Mister Buster" were a close second. Another human that was on the show was Princess Summerfall Winterspring played by Judy Tyler. The mute clown Clarabell was played by three actors. The first was Bob Keeshan, who later became Captain Kangaroo.

Chapter 2

School Days

I remember my first day of Kindergarten as being very scary. My mother walked me to school for several days until I felt confident to go by myself. My teacher, Mrs. Duncan, was very nice to us and would read to the class and play the piano while we sat on the floor. I liked to dig dirt out of the cracks in the floor with the tips of my shoe laces while she read. Sometimes we would build things with huge wooden blocks and play "Billy Goat Gruff." Each day we would take out our small rugs and take a nap on them; very few of us actually went to sleep.

Hall Grade School-Picture taken about 1980

About 25 years ago I came back to St. Joe from Bakersfield, California where I was living at the time, on a vacation and decided to visit my old grade school. I should have gone to the office first but my mind was just floating in fond memories of the past. I went down to the basement to look at the cafeteria and restrooms and then when I walked back up the stairs the Principal met me in the hall and wanted to know what I was doing. I apologized for not going to her office first and told her that I had gone to Hall School starting in about 1944. She then said, "I know who you are!" I said I didn't think she did since it had been many years since I had been there. She said, "You're Larry Flinchpaugh!" A cold chill went over me. I sure didn't recognize her and how could she recognize me? When I had been a student there I had quite a bit more hair than now and of course was quite a bit smaller. She proceeded to explain that I had been in her first class and that she re-membered every one of her students in that class, but later there were just too many to remember. She told me that this was her last year and she would be retiring. We had a nice conversation and I suddenly realized had I waited just a few months, I would have missed this encounter.

See anyone you know? Mickey Lamb, Andy Zipp, Merill Ehlert, Cleo Carr, Jimmie Coy, Larry Flinchpaugh (partial listing)

I don't remember too much about the first grade through the sixth grade but I think I liked recess best and trying to win marbles from my classmates. We would draw a circle in the dirt and try to shoot each other's marbles out of the circle. Our winnings were usually kept in a big sock. I was probably better at climbing the rope in the gym and touching the ceiling than I was at playing marbles. Some of the smarter kids couldn't climb the rope which vindicated me as an 8 or 9 year old having trouble keeping up academically.

I always seemed to have trouble learning in school. My report cards would say "Larry is a good citizen but needs to work harder on his studies." At least I was a good citizen. I don't think I had any serious learning problems but I did learn at a slower rate than some of my classmates. Not all people learn at the same rate but still are grouped in a class that they might not be able to keep up with. Oops. I ended a sentence with a preposition. I think it was Churchill who said, "This is nonsense up with which I will not put!" Our educational system is still slow to recognize that children of the same age do not necessarily learn at the same rate. Maybe it's just too expensive to change the system or they think it will hurt their ego if they group them according to their abilities instead of by age. I would much prefer to see some changes in our educational system, especially in the early grades, than to have to spend so much money on social problems which can follow later.

Like many boys who were "good citizens" I was a patrol boy, helping the other children arrive safely to and from school. Patrol boys were given a badge and white belt plus respect from the teachers and fellow classmates. A few years ago, I bought a patrol badge at a yard sale that was exactly like the one I had at Hall School.

Once a week during my early school years we would walk to the Huffman Memorial church a few blocks away to a Bible study class. My friends in California couldn't believe that Bible study was actually conducted with the approval of the public school system. I remember it as being a little awkward because some of the Jewish and Catholic children did not participate in the classes. I am pretty sure that the kids who did not take part were embarrassed or at least put in an awkward position. People today still say they want religion or at least prayer taught in the school. Even though they have good intentions, they really don't understand the problems this would cause. Their definition of religion is of course the Christian Religion. What they don't realize is that in our Democratic society if we allowed Christian prayer and Christian studies we would have to also allow Muslim, Jewish, Buddhist, etc. prayers and study. I do believe it would be best to leave religious studies to the churches, private schools and the family.

About the time I started into 2nd grade my parents started their business, Flinchpaugh's Pet Shop at eighth and Messanie, so my mother wasn't at home to fix my lunch.. I was afraid to eat in the school cafeteria because I knew I would be embarrassed if I couldn't eat my spinach or some other "icky" food. My mother was very understanding and consequently left a lunch on the kitchen table each day for me. The only problem was that I was afraid to go into the house to eat it when no one else was at home. So I would run in and grab the bag and take it out to the front porch to eat. Luckily this fear wasn't with me forever. I don't remember whether it lasted one year, two, or how many exactly, but by the time I got to Bliss Jr. High I know it was no longer a **problem. I actually thought the school food was quite good by** that time. I loved the sloppy joe sandwiches and the buttered potatoes.

The first thing to do after getting home from school was to read the comics in the newspaper. My favorites were Dick Tracy, Henry, Nancy, and Out Our Way. Next, we listened to our favorite radio programs; Captain Midnight, Sky King, Sgt. Preston of the Yukon and his Dog King, Straight Arrow, Bobby Benson and the B Bar B Riders, and The Green Hornet. I especially remember Ovalteen and Nabisco advertising on these programs. I still remember the Nabisco commercial on Straight Arrow. "N-A-B-I-S-C-0, NABISCO IS THE NAME TO KNOW, FOR A BREAKFAST TREAT THAT YOU CAN'T BEAT, EAT NABISCO SHREDDED WHEAT. STRAIGHT ARROW.....THUD!

Captain Midnight had a secret decoding device that all kids just had to have. You would send 25 cents and a box top for it, and the next day started watching for it in the mail. Those wonderful treasures from cereal companies usually took about 4 weeks to arrive. That was an eternity for a kid. But once I got it I was able to decode the secret messages Captain Midnight would read over the radio. My closest friends and I went on to develop our own code by writing down the alphabet and then substituting numbers or letters next to it to develop a new alphabet that only we knew how to read.

I attended Bliss Jr. High School on Lafayette Street for the 7th and 8th grades. I was still having trouble academically. Not only was I not able to keep up but was continuously being embarrassed by my teachers. If I didn't know the answer to a question, I wouldn't raise my hand but the teachers would call on me anyway. I think that the embarrassment this caused may have hurt me in my future school years. Even today, when I am asked a question, I sometimes interpret it as a threat and then can't concentrate on the correct answer. I have talked to teachers recently

31

and they say that today most teachers understand this problem and are taught not to embarrass the student in this way.

My best friends in Jr. High were Jimmy Coy, Mickey Lamb, Cleo Carr, Richard Tiller and Roger Wilson. Jimmy Coy's father was the principal of Bliss. One morning one of my teachers sent me to the office for something I hadn't done. Luckily, I had stayed all night the night before at Jimmy's house and had had breakfast with Mr. Coy about two hours earlier. Needless to say, I didn't get into any trouble. I explained to him what had happened and after a few minutes of small talk Mr. Coy sent me back to class. I felt pretty good to have friends in such high places!

Cleo Carr's dad was a school shop teacher and helped Cleo and me to build a Tesla coil for a science fair project at Central. Also, Cleo had his grandfather's old Model T Ford in the garage and was restoring it. At the time I didn't think much about the Model T, but years later it was my plan to acquire my own Model T. Now I have two of my own; a 1922 Touring car and a 1923 flatbed truck plus the 1931 Chevrolet Cabriolet that I bought while in high School.

Larry with his 1931 Chevrolet in Central's parking lot. (1957)

The father of my good friend Roger Wilson was a highway patrolman. Around November 1959, I met up him when he was working at an accident near my home north of St. Joe in Country Club Place. I heard a lot of sirens near the highway about four blocks from my house and walked down to the area where the ambulance and patrol cars were and saw Mr. Wilson assisting a tow truck driver attaching a cable to one side of a smashed car. I assumed that the ambulance had already taken the occupants to the hospital. I was wrong. They were still in the car. As the tow truck turned the car right side up I could see that the driver's head was cut off, hanging by only a small piece of skin tissue. His wife's arms and legs were both protruding out the same window. I almost passed out at seeing this gruesome scene.

Later I read that the driver was drunk and left the highway on a curve covered with ice. Apparently he was traveling at a high rate of speed and lost control of his car, hitting the embankment. Not only were the driver and his wife dead at the scene but they were unable to save the pregnant wife's baby. This experience still haunts me to this day. I am sure it has affected the way I drive. I won't ever drive if I have had any alcoholic beverages and I don't like to drive faster than about 65 mph. In fact, I hated to see the 55 MPH speed limit law that went into effect in the 1970s repealed a few years later.

My High School years at Central High School were pretty enjoyable. I had lots of friends, including girl friends, and lots of interests involving old cars, ham radio, flying, astronomy, and working part time for KFEQ TV as "Floor Director." By my junior and senior years it seemed that the teachers were more than just teachers. We seemed more like friends who respected each other. I guess this was a natural part of growing up.

My science teacher was Lecil Carroll who was also a ham radio operator and the manager of the stage crew of which I was a member. I had just gotten my Ham radio license and thought it was nice to have a teacher that was also a Ham radio operator. Roger Wilson was the head of the stage crew and Cleo Carr, David Asbury, Dan Mannschreck and I helped run the sound system and spot lights, and we constructed scenery for school plays.

We had keys to many of the off-limit areas of the school and could always come up with an excuse to be out of class when confronted. I remember carrying a folded blank piece of pink paper that resembled a hall pass. The teachers didn't ever question us as long as we had a pink slip. Also they probably assumed we were working on some type of stage project. We thought we were pretty clever.

We had a secret meeting place about 15 feet above the stage on a scenery storage platform. The only access was by climbing a ladder attached to the wall and crawling through a small opening in the floor of the platform. We even installed a trap door that could be locked from above. The scenery panels were all pushed to the front so we could have a small space at the rear to hold our meetings. We would on occasion invite our girl friends to have lunch with us in our secret hiding place. Anytime a teacher came back stage unexpectedly we would holler out "What time is it?" That was our code that a teacher was present. It worked pretty well. Of course we weren't really doing anything wrong anyway!

A New York play company called "Clare Tree Majors Productions" would put on plays at our high school for the grade school children. I think Alice and Wonderland was one of the plays. Most of the actors played multiple parts and had to make quick costume changes back stage. We thought it was pretty neat to watch the female actresses disrobe and change costumes. We tried not to stare but being teenage boys made that a little difficult.

My algebra teacher was Vance Carroll, Lecil Carroll's cousin. I found out that Vance was working on his pilot's instructor rating so one day asked him if he would teach me to fly. He said that if I would pay for the gas and oil he would give me flying lessons. At that time we could fly for an hour for about $5 worth of gas. Since he didn't yet have his instructor's license it couldn't be counted legally towards my pilot's license, but at least I could learn to fly very cheaply. So, I learned to fly and enjoyed it immensely, but never did solo.

Aeronca Champ Airplane
Note: Our plane didn't even have an electric starter! The instructor/pilot pushed on the brakes while I turned the propeller by hand until it started, which was kind of like starting your lawnmower by turning it upside down and turning the blade with your hands.

My speech teacher was Dorothy Graham. I had a close relationship with her because of my work on the school plays. One day Roger Wilson and I thought it would be fun to play a practical joke on the class. At lunch time we climbed through the class room window and completely turned the entire room around, desks, pictures, etc. After lunch we entered the classroom with every one else and tried to look startled about the change. Mrs. Graham looked at Roger and me and said, "Would you two boys please turn all the furniture back around like it was?" Years later at a class reunion I asked her how she knew it was us. She said she didn't even remember the incident! I thought, "All that work for nothing!"

Mr. Ralph Wilkinson, my COE teacher, helped me get a part time job at KFEQ TV (now KQTV) in 1957, my senior year. It was probably one of the most enjoyable jobs that any kid could have. I would go to work about 2:30 in the afternoon and get off about 10:30 in the evening after the 10 o'clock news. It seemed like long hours for a teenager but it really wasn't. I had time to do my homework between shows and during the commercial breaks.

I would set up scenery props, run the tele-prompter, handle the boom mike, and advise the announcers on the amount of time left to the end of the show, or cue them for a commercial. We had a lot of hand signals that told them what to do. I would give them the signals by holding up my fingers next to camera lens while being very careful to not get into the picture. I had a portable radio receiver attached to my belt so that I could receive instructions from the program director, the lighting director, and the audio director. I thoroughly enjoyed my work at the TV station and my association with the other employees. Most of the technical people were Ham radio operators. Once a week, I would take an animal from my dad's zoo and show it on "Don Berlies" children show.

A lot of funny things happened while I was working for KFEQ. One night, Johnny Yates, the weather man, said that it was going to be pair and fartly cloudy tomorrow. The cameraman, Jack Miller, was laughing so hard and shaking the camera so that the TV picture was moving up and down.

Old Man Jackson was showing the TV viewers how durable the new Formica top kitchen table was. He took a lit cigarette and put it out by pushing it into the Formica top. The camera went in to get a close up of the supposedly undamaged top but instead there was a big burn spot on the table.

As floor director, one of my favorite things to do was develop special effects for the children's show. Since I was interested in magic, I thought it would be fun if I could make Don Berlie disappear while he was standing in front of the set. Before the show went on the air, I took a Polaroid picture of the empty set and placed it on an easel that could be accessed by camera one. Then I had camera 2 focus on the live set. Both cameras were then turned on at the same time so that the pictures could be lined up exactly. When we went on the air and Don said he would disappear on the count of three, we merely transferred the picture from the live set to the Polaroid picture that had been previously taken with no one in the picture. I was looking at the monitor when Don said "Three" and sure enough it looked as if he had really disappeared. In fact some of the office personnel had come down to the viewing room to see how I had made Don disappear. They could see that he was actually still there but the TV monitor showed he had disappeared.

I graduated from Central High School in 1957 and went to KU "Kansas University" in Lawrence, Kansas to major in Electrical Engineering. I had a difficult time with math and chemistry so returned to St. Joseph Junior College and obtained a 2 year Liberal Arts degree. Still interested in electronics, in 1960, I enrolled at Central Technical Institute in Kansas City Missouri. I had just gotten married and going to school and working at the same time was very difficult. I soon found out that I was color blind which made it impossible for me to read values of colored electrical components and was still having difficulty with mathematics so I decided to work on a business degree.

In 1961 I attended night classes at the University of Missouri in Kansas City while working for Phillips Petroleum Company. After Phillips transferred me to Bartlesville, Oklahoma, I attended Tulsa University majoring in Accounting. I didn't graduate from TU but took a correspondence accounting and management course from the "International Accounts Society". For the first time in my life I could learn at my own pace with a correspondence course. Even though I never received a four year college degree, the correspondence course has served me well.

Almost any subject can be designed as a correspondence course and could fill the need for people like me. You just keep doing the same lessons over and over until you completely understand the material. No embarrassment! And no need for anyone to know how long it took. I have often wondered why today's colleges and universities don't take more advantage of correspondent courses. Could it be because the classes would be too efficient and cost effective?

Chapter 3

The Animals in my life

Although I didn't realize it at the time, I had some wonderful experiences with animals in my childhood. My father had always loved animals and I remember him telling me stories of his childhood. As a young child he would take the wooden boxes cheese came in and make them into miniature circus wagons. He would attach four checkers for wheels and add bars on the open side of the box. I would guess that he used nails for the bars. He pretended that the mice caught by the field hands were lions and tigers.

Shortly after getting married, he opened the "Plainview Wild Animal Farm" in Kirksville, Missouri. He charged admission to view the animals and bought and sold animals with the Miller Brothers Circus. I wasn't born until 1939 so only remember the stories and pictures of this part of my father's life.

While growing up, my dad took me to almost every circus that came within 100 miles of St. Joe. He knew most of the owners through his buying and selling of wild animals. Also in the early 1930's during the depression, he worked for a circus taking care of the animals, while my mother made cotton candy. I think my mother was always a little hesitant to talk about the hard times of this period and the fact that they had to work on a traveling circus to make ends meet while my dad thoroughly enjoyed the experience.

The two circuses I remember were "Miller Brothers" (now called Carson and Barnes) that wintered in Hugo Oklahoma and the "Cole Brothers" Railroad Show. The names of the

Miller Brothers Circus owners were Obert Miller and his sons Kelly and Dory. My dad was very good friends with the Miller family and I know had a lot of respect for their business operation. Dad had first met Obert when he started his animal farm in Kirksville in the early 1930's. We always got the best seats in the house when we visited them; usually on the band stand next to the tents entry for the performers. Sometimes we would eat with the performers and crew members. This was quite an experience for me as a child to be that close to all those talented and interesting people from all over the world-acrobats, jugglers, the tattooed lady, the giant man, clowns, and magicians. We would usually arrive at the circus lot early in the morning to watch the elephants erect the huge tents. The circus lot in St. Joe was usually set up at 6th and Atchison Street. In just a few hours the former empty lot was turned into a miniature city of tents, wagons, exotic animals and concession stands.

Even after all these years I can feel the excitement and remember the smells and sounds of the circus lot. First I remember the smell of the fresh cut hay on the field and the animals in the cages. The sounds of the roaring lions and the trumpets of the elephants are still vivid in my mind. And of course the smell and sound of the concession machines. The cotton candy and candy apples were fun to eat but awfully messy.

My dad's relationship with the Miller brothers, Dory, Kelly and their father Obert, would extend well up into the 1960's. When my sister Jean was about twelve she was allowed to ride on top of one of the elephant's heads as it paraded around the Big Top at the beginning of the show.

Every 2-3 years they would send us a baby lion cub which I always tried to tame. It wasn't as easy as it appears in the movies. I was never successful in training a lion that could be trusted around people when it was fully grown. The first one we gave raw horsemeat to eat and the second we made sure the cub didn't get any raw bloody meat. It didn't seem to make any difference. Even the small cubs would hiss and try to bite you while putting on a collar and chain. I finally strung the chain through a 3 foot piece of pipe so I could keep the cub far enough away from me so he couldn't knock me over with a swipe of his paw. I decided that the lions in the movies are probably bred for several years with the tamest cubs of each litter to develop a tamer animal. I suspect that some of them in the movies are also partially sedated while they are performing.

Johnny Flinchpaugh   *A Dandy Lion*   *Pepper Shady age 11*

Training a lion wasn't anything like training a chimpanzee. All you had to do with Vicky was to show her how to do something and she would just copy you. I showed her one time how to jump on a pogo stick and she did it right the first time.

One time we went to the Cole Brothers circus and my dad had business with the owner before the show started. The owner's office was in a railroad car connected to another rail car housing a gambling casino just for the circus help. The owner gave me a hand full of nickels to play the slot machines while he and my dad conducted business. By the time we were ready to leave, I had won about $20.00. Since slots were illegal in Missouri at the time, none of my friends at school the next day believed I had really played the slot machines the night before.

Larry and his Scottie," Frisky" c. 1942 in the front yard at 2614 Duncan street

My first dog was a black Scottie named Dina and when she died we kept one of her puppies named Frisky. I was pretty young but do remember the comfort I got from talking to Frisky when no one else would listen or understand. She always listened intently and somehow everything got better. I was very sad when our veterinarian, Dr. Bailey, had to put her to sleep. Later we got a fox terrier named Midget and after that, in about 1953, Missouri Congressman William C. Cole gave us his Schnauzer named Bobo since he couldn't take him to Washington DC.

The pet shop my dad opened at 603 South 8th Street in St. Joe in 1946 had a large variety of animals. Jocko was the monkey I remember best. I think he was a cinnamon ringtail. We also had lots of dogs, cats, parrots, canaries, parakeets, turtles, lizards, etc. My dad had a pretty good since of humor. A lady came into the shop one day and wanted to sell him a dog for $50.00 that was probably worth only about $10.00. Without hesitating my dad said, "I can't pay you $50.00 for your dog but I would be willing to trade you for those two $25.00 cats in the front window." I thought this was pretty funny since the cats were worth about $10.00. I don't think that the lady even caught on that he was kidding her.

Ben Magoons Delicatessen was at the south end of block across the street from our pet shop. We used to get the best pastrami sandwiches on black pumpernickel bread and potato salad from them. Even after we moved the pet shop to 1202 Frederick we would often return there to eat. We had lots of excellent eating places in St. Joe in those days. The Bucket Shop in South St. Joe, Wades Indian Grill on Frederick Ave across from the Uptown Theatre, and Jerri Ann's Cafeteria near our house were other favorites. My dad used to get brain sandwiches at Wades. It made me sick to even think about a brain sandwich. My dad even ate pig's feet.

Believe it or not, we usually drank water with our meals instead of a coke. A coke was reserved for the movies or a special treat at home on Saturday night while listing to Fibber McGee and Molly or the "Great Gildersleve" on the radio. Not only that, the bottles were only 6.5 ounces and a small glass full of ice at the drug store fountain made a suitable serving size. Big Gulps had not been invented yet. We even bought ice cream in pint size cartons and cut it with a sharp knife into slices that would feed all four of us in the family. Do you suppose there is any connection to our weight problems today with our eating habits?

For some unknown reason, I would sit on the floor and stare into the radios speaker. The mental picture of what was happening on the radio seemed to be better that way.

The Great Guildersleeve Show was another favorite. Many of these shows can be heard today on "Sirius" satellite radio or found on the internet.

The first thing the kids would do after getting out of school was to hurry home to listen to the radio serials.

The Fibber McGee and Molly radio show was one of the most popular radio shows in the late 1940's and early 50's- like the Seinfeld TV show is today.

About four doors south of our pet shop on 8th Street was a junk shop that had just about anything you could want. It was crammed from floor to ceiling with antiques and junk. The owner, Mr. Cook, always had a 4 or 5 day beard, dirty fingernails and overalls with holes in the knees. But he had a huge diamond ring on his left hand and his overall pockets were always filled with a large wad of bills. This was my first lesson not to judge people on how they looked. This probably influenced me later in life to see the value in used items and antiques when I subsequently opened a personal property liquidating business in 1981 in Bakersfield, California. (Consign It Stores, Inc.)

In 1951 my parents purchased the old Hartsock Hospital Building at 1202 Frederick Ave in St. Joe and moved the pet shop from 8th Street to Frederick. We sold our house at 2614 Duncan Street and moved on to the second floor of the pet shop. My bedroom was on the third floor next to an apartment we rented out.

My dad bought me a used bike so I could ride to Bliss Junior High School. Sometime later I won a new bike from the Kitty Clover Potato Chip Co. by appearing on WDAF TV in Kansas City with a Coati Mundi from the pet Shop. I asked my dad what to do if the coati mundi bit me on live TV. He said, "Just put your hand in your pocket." Since we didn't have color TV at that time, I guess that it wouldn't have made any difference.

In about 1955 my parents bought the Pony Express Reptile Gardens on Frederick Ave (Hwy 36 East of the Belt Hwy) from the man he had managed it for, Nick Nickerson, and the real estate property from his old friend Carl Johnston from Kirksville, Missouri. The property had earlier been used as a roller skating rink by Carl. Carl had leased it to

Nick Nickerson after moving his skating rink about one half mile West on Frederick (now a furniture store). Nick Nickerson also owned Nickerson Appliances in South St. Joe. After selling the Reptile Gardens to my dad, Nick opened another one in Eldon Missouri. At the time of this writing this property is now the home of "The Citizens Bank and Trust Company" on Frederick which looks across the street at the "East Hills Shopping Center."

The building at 1202 Frederick was sold to Reynolds Boat Shop which had been next door to the pet shop and the pet shop was moved to the reptile gardens. At that time there was a small airport behind the reptile gardens and a large corn field across the highway owned by Mr. Farber. The corn field is now The East Hills Mall. The old pet shop building at 12th and Frederick was torn down a few years after being sold by my parents

(Left) Vicky teasing the puppies (Right) one of dads many circus friends, Ada Szasz with her trained bear.

I remember the interesting visits of the circus performers to our house. They taught me how to juggle, walk on my hands and various magic tricks. One of my favorite teachers was Chinese. His name was Foo Ling Yu. (joke) These are fond memories that I cherish to this day. I still enjoy doing magic tricks for both children and adults. While living in California I belonged to the "Magic Circle" club.

Vicky showing off her skating abilities.

Aerial view of the Reptile Gardens at 3727 Frederick. Across the highway was Mr. Farbers corn field which today is the East Hills Shopping Center. Texaco & Standard Oil Service Stations were directly West of the reptile gardens.

47

An airport was behind the reptile gardens. (North) The water tower, in the upper rightof the picture on the previous page is near the 'Cool Crest" miniature golf course. "Firestone" is now directly east of the old reptile gardens site.

The old highway 36 went right by the reptile gardens. I have been told that it used to be called, "The Ocean to Ocean Highway." We had vistors from almost every state in the union.There were signs, similar to the Burma shave signs, adverising the reptile gardens all the way to Hamilton.

A "white"' black bear cub in front of the reptile gardens and zoo.

There was a corn crib at the front and on the east side of the parking lot that housed two full grown black bears. My dad told a new employee to feed the bears some of the day old donuts we had picked up at Safeway. A few minutes later my dad looked out the window and could see that instead of poking the donuts through a "feeding opening" in the cage, the employee was actually inside the cage handing the bears one donut at a time. My dad couldn't believe this.

He hollored at him and told him to get out of the cage immediately. "The bears are going to be really mad when you run out of donuts and may attack you."

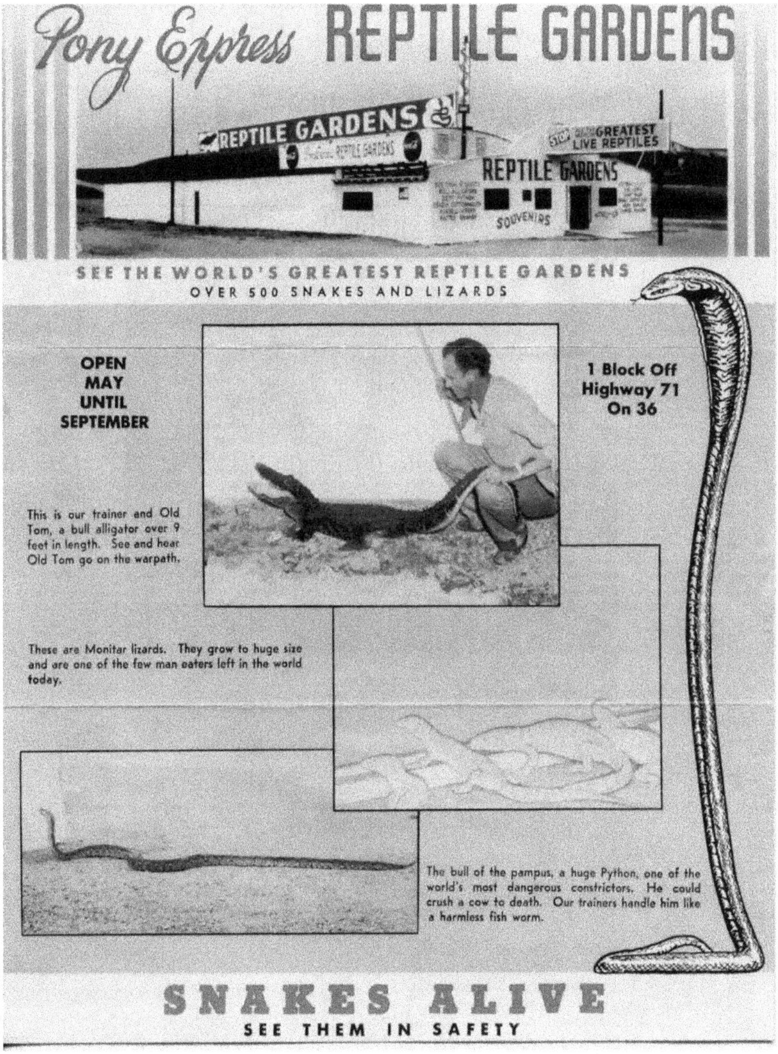

Pony Express REPTILE GARDENS

REPTILE GARDENS

GREATEST LIVE REPTILES

REPTILE GARDENS

SOUVENIRS

SEE THE WORLD'S GREATEST REPTILE GARDENS
OVER 500 SNAKES AND LIZARDS

OPEN
MAY
UNTIL
SEPTEMBER

1 Block Off
Highway 71
On 36

This is our trainer and Old Tom, a bull alligator over 9 feet in length. See and hear Old Tom go on the warpath.

These are Monitor lizards. They grow to huge size and are one of the few man eaters left in the world today.

The bull of the pampas, a huge Python, one of the world's most dangerous constrictors. He could crush a cow to death. Our trainers handle him like a harmless fish worm.

SNAKES ALIVE
SEE THEM IN SAFETY

My father, Johnny Flinchpaugh was first the manager of the "Pony Express Reptile Gardens owned by Nick Nickerson before he purchased the property and added his own pet shop and zoo.

The east side airport was directly behind the Reptile Gardens. When taking off from the airport you had to be alert and not run into KFEQ's TV tower.

"Yeah ,Yeah, I know I look silly in a dress. I am just monkeying around. What do you think I am- a cheap skate?"

"Would you believe I can tie my own shoes?
Well, I can't. My assistant does that for me."

Chapter Four

Vicky Lynn
Star of Stage, TV, Screen and the Movies

(Krug Park Bowl—KFEQ TV—Harvard Film)

Our Chimpanzee, Vicky Lynn, was the most memorable animal in my life. I even hesitate to call her an animal. Even though she wasn't human she was pretty close to it. I have never seen an animal with this degree of intelligence. She could duplicate almost anything you would show her. At least she could do the things that a small child could do. Even doctor Hughes remarked how similar she was to a human when he was caring for her. She was like a movie star in St. Joe and was constantly in the newspaper, appeared on television, performed at the Krug Park Bowl and did daily performances at our reptile gardens and zoo.

One day a lady tried to get a Coke from our coke machine and was having difficulty in spite of the fact that the directions were plainly printed on the door. It said, (1) "Deposit dime, (2) pull handle down, (3) open door and remove bottle." The lady just couldn't seem to follow those simple directions. So I said, "Give Vicky your dime." Vicky promptly put the dime in her teeth so it would match the direction of the coin slot. She then dropped the dime into the slot, pulled the handle down, opened the door, and removed the bottle. I looked at the lady and said, "See, anybody can do it." She didn't think that was very funny. Vicky didn't either and of course wanted to keep the Coke for herself. Vicky naturally thought the Coke was for her and not the lady. So I promptly bought another bottle for the lady.

We had a kitchen at the Reptile Gardens where my mother would often cook there instead of at our home for our personal meals. In the morning before opening, I would let Vicky out of her cage to run loose through the entire building. One morning I heard my mother scream and the kitchen door slam. As I ran to the front of the building, I saw Vicky running out of the kitchen with an angel food cake covered in white fluffy frosting under one arm and poking huge chunks of it into her mouth as she was running. She soon consumed the whole cake! Vicky didn't even get into trouble as everyone thought it was funny, even my mother. If I had done that when I was Vicky's age, I would have been in big trouble.

I tried to teach Vicky table manners but to no avail. She would have breakfast with us sitting at the same table and eating her cereal with a spoon. She liked to put one toe on the edge of the table while she ate. I never could teach her that this behavior wasn't polite. Then one morning she grabbed a whole quarter pound cube of butter and ate it like a popsicle. It almost made me sick watching her eat the entire cube but I wasn't about to take it away from her. By this time she weight about 60 pounds and was very capable of protecting her rights.

I always thought it would be interesting if she could talk. Apparently there is something lacking in a chimpanzee's vocal chords and brain that doesn't allow this even though they have the ability to think like a human. Years later I got the idea of teaching her sign language after watching a PBS program. Dr. Roger Foust of the University of Oklahoma was teaching chimps' how to communicate using sign language. The chimps were able to learn several hundred words and even to put words together to express simple ideas. One chimp signed for a piece of rock candy meaning he wanted a piece of hard candy. As an airplane flew over, one of the chimps signed that it wanted to ride in the flying car. I wrote Dr. Fouts and he sent me some of his research papers but by this time I had already moved away from home and Vicky had died. I think she was about 27 years old when she died in Muscatine, Iowa at the Weed Park Zoo where my dad Johnny was zoo superintendent. Just think, if I had taught Vicky sign language, I could have asked her if she believed in evolution or some other earth shattering question. What a contribution to science that would have been.

Another example illustrating her intelligence was when I was playing catch with her and she spotted a bunch of grapes on a table about 10 feet from the stool she was sitting on. She wanted the grapes in the worst way but I told her not to leave the stool. She promptly looked around, and then threw the ball down the hall away from me and the grapes. I knew what she had in mind and I wanted to reward her for being so smart. After retrieving the ball and getting back to her, it appeared she hadn't left the stool. However, the grapes were gone and her mouth was so full of grapes she could hardly hide them. Grapes and grape juice were oozing from her mouth.

One of the funniest things happened when Vicky pulled a Kleenex from the box and instantly another one popped up. Humans understand this but Vicky was intrigued at how fast another Kleenex would replace the one she had just pulled from the box. She almost emptied the entire box before I could get her to stop.

There were always people who teased Vicky but she would get even with them. Once she was eating from a bag of peanuts that had been thrown into her cage. She offered a small boy a peanut just as someone had done to her earlier but as soon as he reached out to take it, she jerked it back; just like a youngster had done to her earlier. Animals do have a since of humor.

Vicky was so strong that she was able to break out of her cage by twisting and turning the pieces of her wire enclosure until there was a hole large enough for her to escape. Once she escaped and we found her in the back room washing the python snake cage window with a dirty sponge that Bill White had left on the floor when he had gone to lunch.

I was constantly trying experiments with her just to see how intelligent she was. I had always heard that man was the only animal capable of making and using tools. I discovered that wasn't true back in 1956 before PBS later showed a chimp using a stick to get ants out of an ant hill.

We kept the key to Vicky's cage hanging about four feet from her cage on a nail. I gave her a yard stick to see if she would even think about using it as a tool to reach the key. She played with the yard stick for a few minutes and then a light went on in her head. She stuck the yardstick out the side of the cage and immediately used it to knock the key off the nail and on to the floor. She then used the yardstick to drag the key over to the cage where she was able to pick it up. She was able to put the key into the lock but she didn't realize that it had to be turned to open the lock.

I was taking a psychology class in 1959 at the St. Joseph Junior College when I asked the instructor if she would like me to bring a chimp to class the next day and give the class a demonstration on how smart they are. Not believing that I actually had a chimp, she said, "ok sure." The very next day I came walking into the class with Vicky carrying my books and me holding her other hand. Vicky shook hands with everyone and threw them all a kiss and performed a few of her tricks. I said, "Vicky, clap you hands", which she did. I then said, "Vicky, applause." She just looked at me because she had never heard the word "applause." I showed her about four times that "applause" meant the same as "clap your hands." I gave her an apple and waited about 15 minutes to see if she would pass the test. With my hands at my side I said, "Vicky, "applause." She thought for a second than clapped her hands. It worked. This was a live demonstration that proved exactly how intelligent chimps are.

Like any young child, Vicky enjoyed riding in the car. One afternoon I took her with my wife and me to the downtown post office to pick up the mail. As I stepped out of the car, I gave Phyllis the pistol, loaded with blanks, and told her if in the unlikely event she needed to, she could use it to protect herself. Phyllis dropped the pistol between the seats and was unable to retrieve it. Vicky promptly stuck her smaller hand between the seats and picked it up and handed the loaded pistol to Phyllis. Phyllis wondered if Vicky might shoot her but fortunately she did not.

A few months later when she was about 7 years old, she went into an extreme tantrum mode and attacked me while I was putting her back into her cage. She reached through the bars trying to bite me while screaming and showing her teeth. Luckily I had a 32 pistol loaded with blanks in my back pocket and after shooting her in the stomach six times, she let me go. The hair on her stomach was almost completely burned off from the powder burns. She was sorry and wanted to kiss me to make up but of course I couldn't take a chance of being attacked after this temper tantrum.

I was extremely saddened that she had done this and from that time on I was acutely aware of how dangerous she could be. I rarely took her out of her cage after that. Recently there have been stories in the papers and on TV about chimps seriously wounding someone; usually a friend. They, like any wild animal, must be handled with great care and a sense of what they are capable of doing.

Vicky was extremely gentle when she was young, almost like a human child. But when she was about six and maturing, she entered an age of more tantrums and because of her growing size and extreme strength had to be watched more closely. She was always sorry after one of her tantrums, but we knew we had to be very alert when we had her out of her cage at that age.

Congressman Cole gave Larry his dog "Bobo" when he went to Washington DC. Each year Bobo would get a Christmas card from Washington.

Johnny Flinchpaugh with a South American "Tapir."

"I don't remember it being this cold in Africa."

57

"This is much more fun than shoveling snow and besides, don't I look pretty"

Vicky was so used to having her picture taken-- she actually would pose for the picture like a small child. Her antics were recorded in the late 1950's and early 1960's by hundreds of visitors to the reptile gardens on their 8mm movie cameras.

A few years ago, Dr. Hughes' wife gave me a copy of her 8mm film showing Vicky doing one of her Sunday afternoon shows. Of course the quality of the 8mm film is not as good as today's digital cameras but it is nice to have a moving picture copy of this part of my life with Vicky. This short 8mm movie of Vicky can be viewed on my web site at www.larryflinchpaugh.com

Chapter Five
My Job

From the time I was 12 or 13, I worked for my father in his animal business. One of my first jobs was to clean the puppy pens. I got very good at tearing newspaper into long strips for bedding but never did like removing all the pee soaked papers.

Our pet shop on 8th Street was only about four or five blocks south of the main downtown area and about two miles from our home at 2614 Duncan Street. There was a Safeway store directly across the street where the store manager would save the fruit and bread that was to be thrown out for our animals. I even ate some of the animals' food. This was probably my first lesson on what it meant to be thrifty. When my dad would buy something that came in a wooden box or we got a wooden orange crate, it was my job to take them apart and save all the boards and nails. I would straighten the nails by hammering them against the cement floor and then put them in a big fruit jar. My dad taught me not to waste anything. This was probably due to his experiencing shortages during the depression and World War II.

It was fun to go to the shop and play with the animals. The first monkey I remember was named Jocko but the one I had the most fun with was "Topper". I think he was a white faced capuchin. *(Reference the front cover)* Topper received a lot of attention when he and I were in the Apple Blossom parade about 1948. Topper was riding on my shoulder during the parade and at the very beginning of the parade he peed and expelled down the inside of my shirt. I was very uncomfortable, but did manage to walk the entire parade in this condition.

In other years when I just "watched" the parade, it was sometimes difficult to get a front row position to see everything. I discovered that if I carried a snake with me, the people in front would just sort of make an opening for me to pass. I thought this was a pretty clever way to get to the front of the crowd and to a prime location to view the parade.

Although I wasn't afraid of snakes, I still had a lot of respect for them. I can't remember ever being bitten by one but that's probably because I never picked up one that I knew wasn't friendly. The friendliest was the Indigo snake and the hog nose snake. The hog nose snake would play dead to confuse his predators. If you picked him up and then laid him back down he would turn over on his back so as to make you believe he was dead. As soon as you would turn him right side up, he would immediately turn over and play dead again. If I picked up a black snake or bull snake or some other snake that was aggressive, I usually wore gloves. Any time I picked up a rattle snake or copper head, I used a snake hook. We made our own snake hooks by removing the end of a golf club and attaching a "u" shaped piece of metal on the end. Another type was just a rope threaded thru a 3 foot piece of pipe. This allowed us to have an adjustable loop at the end of the stick to tighten over the head of the snake.

My dad didn't actually give me an allowance but would allow me to work and he paid me accordingly. When I became a teenager, if I needed extra money, I would sometimes keep the zoo open a couple hours later than usual and my dad let me keep the admission ticket revenue and any pet store sales or gift item sold went to him. It was really a good deal for me to have a ready source of money any time I needed it. In fact when my wife and I were first married and very low on funds, we often kept the reptile gardens open after hours on Friday and Saturday nights. My wife Phyllis would work the admission booth unless young girls came in- in which case Phyllis would go work in the pet shop area and I would work the ticket window. One evening Phyllis and I, in just one hour, collected enough money to go to "Heinies" steak house on the Belt for supper and then take in a movie.

Sample Price List for Animals in the 1950's

Parrots
Mexican and Panama Double Yellow Heads
(good talkers)............. $100.00 to $150.00
McCaw...................................$250.00
Mexican Red Heads.................... .$50.00 up

Dwarf or Half Moons....................$50.00 ea

Cockatiels'
Mated Pairs...............................$35.00
Single Birds...............................$20.00

Monkey_....................$50.00 to $150.00 ea
Chimpanzees...........................$1,000.00 +

White rats...............................$2.00 pair
Hamsters..................................3.00 pair
Baby raccoons..........................$15.00 ea
Baby Alligators..........................$3.00 ea
Chameleons............................50 cents ea

Besides taking tickets, training the animals and cleaning pens, I would give tours of the Reptile Gardens and Zoo for school groups. Even though I wasn't fond of handling the snakes, I still had to handle some and allow the guests to touch them and sometimes they even put them around their neck. As previously said, my two favorite snakes were the indigo (shown below) and the hog nose snake. I don't thank you could make the hognose bite.

This nice non-aggressive Indigo snake is the largest non-venomous snake in North America. Indigo snakes are protected at the state level in Alabama, and have full protection as a threatened species in Florida and Georgia, and as an endangered species in South Carolina and Mississippi.

One time Doctor Deming and another veterinarian had to cut off a chain from around our buffalo's neck because it had opened up a wound. The other vet jumped on the head of the buffalo, holding on to the horns for dear life, while Dr. Deming cut the chain. Of course the buffalo didn't like this and threw the vet off and inadvertently took a slice out of his forehead with a horn. Instead of going to the hospital, Dr. Deming had him sit on the ground while he stitched up the wound. A few months later you couldn't even see a scar on the vet's forehead. All **I** had to do was spray the wound on the buffalo with a sanitized spray.

"Alfonso" the Buffalo-no chain now!

Tame hognose snake-note the upturned snout. They are notorious for playing dead when threatened. This particular variety is predominantly found in the United States and northern Mexico.

It was my job to drain the dirty water and remove the dead fish that the alligators didn't eat. This alligators is probably wondering if I taste like chicken.

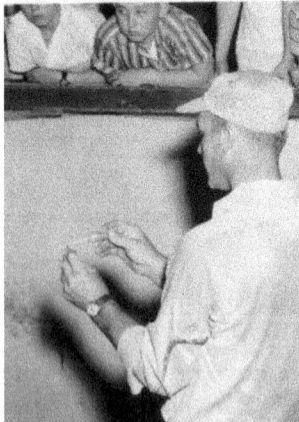

Bill White shown here is milking a rattle snake. This was one job I refused to do.

Chapter Six
Flight for Life

One section of the reptile gardens was devoted to the poisonous snakes which included a king cobra that was about 12 foot long, three Indian cobras, coral snakes, and bushmasters. Once a customer wanted to know why we didn't have the blue racers in the poisoness snake section. My dad explained to them that blue racers were not poisoness but they would not believe him. My dad then opened the door to the cage and stuck his hand into the pile of snakes. Sure enough two of them bit him on the hand causing a small amount of blood to flow. My dad then said, "How long do you think I have to live?" I wasn't about to prove a point using this method while conducting my tours.

Often times we talked about what we would do if any of us were to get bitten by the cobras. I didn't even want to think about that. In fact I often wished that we didn't have any poisonous snakes on display. Today there are special permits needed to have these poisonous snakes. It was my understanding that if you were bitten by a cobra, you would be paralyzed in just a matter of a few minutes and would die. There was anti-venom developed by Bill Hasst of the Miami Serpentarium but few private zoos had it on hand. We were extremely careful to make sure that a tragedy didn't occur while we were handling the cobras.

However, one Sunday afternoon in August, 1959 while 20-30 people were touring the Reptile Gardens, my dad came running up to the front ticket office and whispered that Bill White, our snake handler, had just been bitten by the cobra, and that the cobra **had not** been put back into its cage. As my dad and Bill ran out the door to go to the hospital which was about 3 miles away, I thought, what should I do? All I could think of was that Bill might die and that people touring the Reptile Gardens could be in great danger if the cobra was not put back into its cage. So I rushed to the back room, trying not to look too excited and panic the customers, and told everyone that a black snake had escaped and that they should evacuate the building immediately for their safety. The cobra pen's door was open and the sack used to hold the snake while the pen was being cleaned was on the floor with the handle twisted around the sack opening. I wasn't sure if the snake was <u>under</u> the sack or <u>in</u> the sack. I proceeded to cautiously take a snake hook and very gently raised the sack slightly above the ground. I determined that at least the cobra was not under the sack and was therefore in the sack. About that same time the snake struck the inside of the sack so I knew he was inside. I very gingerly picked up the sack using the snake hook and threw the snake into the cage, sack and all, and slammed the door and locked it.

Now what should I do? I was probably in a state of shock because as I called the police departments to have them escort my dad and Bill to the hospital. I could hardly talk. I finally managed to blurt out **Reptile Gardens, cobra bite, escort to hospital!** Then it occurred to me that I should go get Bill's wife and inform her about the accident and take her to the hospital to be with her husband. I drove to her home, knocked on the door and immediately upon seeing me she asked, "Has Bill been bitten by the cobra?" I don't know how she knew except that I must have looked pretty awful. As we were headed to the hospital, a St. Joseph police officer pulled his motorcycle along side our company truck and said to follow him and he would escort us to the hospital. I shouted out the window that we weren't the one bitten but thanks. We arrived at the hospital a few minutes later to find Bill experiencing some tightness in his joints. Dr Dumont explained that he didn't really know how to treat a patient who had been bitten by a cobra other than to have an iron lung on standby in case Bill could no longer breathe on his own. My dad explained to the doctor that the expert on cobra bites was Bill Hasst, owner of the Miami Serpentarium in Miami, Florida.

The doctor had the nurse call Mr. Hasst but the telephone operator said all the lines were busy. The doctor grabbed the phone and told the operator, "This is Doctor Dumont and this is a matter of life and death!" The phone rang a couple of times and the doctor was talking to Mr. Hasst. After being on hold for about 10 minutes, Mr. Hasst came back on the line and said that he had called the Homestead air base just a few miles from him. He advised us that the air force was sending a helicopter to pick up the anti-venom and that a T33 jet trainer would fly it from Miami, Florida to St. Joseph, Mo., a distance of about 1300 miles, and would arrive in about 3 hours and 48 minutes. The pilots were air force Lts. James H. Ahmann of Louisville, Ky. and Larry Marks of Miami.

I can't remember why, but I was sitting in the back seat of the police car as we waited near the runway at Roscrans Field for the jet to arrive with the anti-venom.

We heard the airport tower announce that the jet was passing over Kansas City about 50 mile away and a minute later it was landing next to the police car at the airport. By this time there was a big crowd of spectators and a lot of newspaper people witnessing this life saving flight. As the canopy on the T33 slid back the flashes of the cameras almost blinded everyone while the policeman grabbed a small box and jumped into his patrol car. We started speeding towards highway 36 and had to pass over the Missouri/Kansas Bridge. The highway patrol had stopped all traffic for several miles in both directions so that we could pass over the bridge into St. Joe without any interference. As we were speeding up 8th street at 60 miles an hour, I was watching the buildings fly by my window, and the driver looked like he was pumping the steering wheel and was looking from side to side with almost a panicked expression. Again, I asked myself, did I really need to be in the police car going at this high rate of speed! But it was too late to get out so I just closed my eyes and prayed we wouldn't hit anyone or anything.

As we arrived at the hospital the officer bolted up the stairs, not waiting for an elevator, to the second floor and gave the anti-venom to the doctor. The doctor told us about an hour later that he thought Bill would be all right. After all the excitement had died down we went back and analyzed what had happened. Apparently the cobra had bitten Bill through the sack and the majority of the snake's venom had been absorbed by the sack itself and very little got into Bill's blood stream. A few months later the cobra died, probably the result of injuring its teeth when it bit through the heavy canvas bag.

This story was distributed by the Associated Press and therefore appeared in newspapers around the world. That night, as I was going home about midnight I tuned across the AM radio dial in my car and heard several stations say, "Heroic Air Force flight saves cobra bite victim in St. Joseph, Missouri". It was quite a memorable experience to have been a part of a story such as this. Thankfully, this story had a happy ending.

JET DELIVERS SERUM

Man Bitten by 4-Foot Cobra May Recover

By Associated Press

St. Joseph, Mo.---A 4 foot long Indian cobra bit an employee of a reptile garden near here yesterday. But he may live because of a dramatic 1,300 mile flight from Miami, Florida.

The Coast Guard and the Air Force flew anti-cobra serum from Miami, Florida to St. Joseph, after 32-year old William White was bitten. The serum was administered 6 hours after the accident.

A single drop of cobra venom can be fatal. Usually it takes only four hours to kill, said William H, Haast, operator of the Miami Serpentarium.

But the cobra's fangs pierced a sack of heavy material before they hit White on the thumb. The bag apparently absorbed some of the venom.

A hospital attendant said White, who has been bitten about 100 times by non-poisoness snakes during his four years at the reptile garden, remarked as the serum was injected:

"I knew all the time I'd be ok."

At mid morning, White appeared to be in good condition.

"He has a chance to recover," said Dr. Dumont. "I think he will be ok."

The doctor said "White has experienced some symptoms of cobra poisoning—particularly stiffing of the joints in his legs and low blood pressure.

At Whites bedside was his wife, Ruby. They have a daughter, Joy, 10 and a son, Robin, 5.

The owner of the reptile garden, John Flinchpaugh, said Whites job was caring for the snakes. Using a long instrument with forceps on one end, White had put the cobra in the heavy bag preparatory to cleaning its cage. It was a routine procedure—a job he had done many times.

After White was bitten, a telephone call was made to the Miami Serpentarium. Flinchpaugh said it was the only source of anti-cobra venom in the United States. The serum is made in Bombay, India.

While Air Force Lts. James H, Ahmann of Louisville, Kentucky and Larry Marks of Miami stood by a T33 jet trainer, a Coast Guard helicopter picked up the vial of serum at the serpentarium. Miami police blocked traffic off a highway so the copter could set down beside the serpentarium. From there, the helicopter made a 15-minute hop to the air base.

The jet covered the 1,300 mile from Miami to this city in northwest Missouri in 3 hours and 48 minutes, including a stop for fuel at Greenville, Mississippi.

Note: Similar news stories appeared in Newspapers throughout the world. The irony of this story is that the cobra died and the snake bite victim, Bill White, survived. The Minneapolis Star newspaper, as well as numerous other papers, carried the follow-up story as shown on the next page.

THE MINNEAPOLIS STAR
Wednesday September 2, 1959

Victim Lives- Cobra Dies

ST. JOSEPH, Mo.—(AP) Two weeks ago a deadly hooded cobra from India bit a reptile garden snake handler, William White.

Anti-cobra serum was flown here from Miami, Florida in Air Force jets and White, 38, recovered.

John Flinchpaugh, operator of the reptile gardens said the snakes fangs were loosened when it struck through a heavy canvas bag to bite White. Its jaw was dislocated when White jerked his hand away.

Death was attributed to infection of the injured area. The injury wasn't discovered until several days ago.

No one seemed interested in trying to reset the jaw.

Note: The picture on the next page was our first chimp that died from pneumonia. I have often wondered if she caught a virus from one of the hundreds of people who visited our pet shop to enter the contest to give her a name. I remember almost everyone wanted to touch her.

Young chimps at this early age are especially prone to catch germs from humans before there immune system is fully developed.

71

Our first chimp that died from pneumonia

Chapter Seven
Visiting the Farm

Almost ever summer I would visit my Uncle Clyde Tomlin, Aunt Winnie, Cousin Mike and Grandmother Wilson in Breckenridge, Missouri. Breckenridge is only about 60 miles from St. Joseph but it took over 4 hours to make the trip by train. My mom and dad would take me to the Union train depot on Sixth Street about 8 o'clock in the evening to board the Burlington train and I would arrive in Breckenridge about 12:00 midnight. It took so long because the train had to wait in Cameron, Mo for the west bound train from Chicago to pass.

I have fond memories of the old Union train depot on south 6th street. It was such an exciting place in the 1940's and 50's, probably like the Kansas City International Airport is today. The sights, sounds and smells are still vivid in my mind. The depot was full of servicemen and people from all walks of life busily boarding the trains. I think the Burlington was the main passenger train serving our area. I can still hear the sounds coming from the big speakers announcing arrivals and departures. "All------------- a---------------------board----------------for------------- Chicago now leaving on track five." The sound echoed thru the huge terminal. The smell of cigars and cigarettes was so heavy you could hardly breathe at times. There were spittoons (Cuspidors) so people could spit their tobacco juice into them. I remember seeing ladies with rubber gloves and a small brush cleaning them. Even as a small child, I thought it was disgusting. There were stain marks all over the floor around each spittoon where people missed their target. In the 1940's and 50's smoking and chewing tobacco was an ac-

73

cepted practice. A few years later not only were the spittoons removed but also the ashtrays. There are still people who smoke and chew today but it is no longer accepted by the general public. The movie industry still tries to get the public to smoke by showing cool and famous people smoking. They must receive secret payments from the tobacco companies to continue the myth that tobacco is not harmful to your health. It appears that they are more interested in profits than what is best for the American people.

It was fascinating to see all the things for sale at the magazine and candy counter. Every kind of candy and magazine you could think of was available. I always wanted to load up with things for my long four hour trip. My mother would instruct the conductor to look after me and make sure I got off in Breckenridge, Missouri and not continue on to Chicago, Illinois.

The train was really old even for the 1940's. The engine was coal fired and you could raise the windows and stick your head out. That was fine as long as the train was going straight ahead but when it turned on a long curve you would get a face full of soot from the engine.

The passenger car looked exactly like the train cars used in the old western movies. There was a wood heating stove at both ends and a brass suitcase rack on both sides running the entire length of the train car. The seats had a Victorian look and were very uncomfortable. Looking back, the train cars were probably built about 1890.

I remember once the conductor told me that there weren't enough people getting off in Breckenridge so the train wouldn't stop. He said I would have to jump off as the train slowed down. I figured he was kidding, but wasn't really sure. Fortunately, they stopped long enough for me to get off.

Uncle Clyde, Aunt Winnie and Mike would pick me up about mid-night and we would drive to their farm 3 miles west of Breckenridge.

Early post card of Union Station on south 6th.
It looked pretty much like this in the late 1940's

Breckenridge Missouri depot
Originally the "Hannibal & St. Joseph" Railroad. Later it be-
came the "Chicago, Burlington & Quincy (CB&Q) Railroad."

The next morning we would get up at the crack of dawn. No need for an alarm clock! The roosters would let you know when it was time to get up.

I couldn't believe how much work there was to be done on the farm. I was from the city and played with the animals at my dad's zoo more than I worked. Farm life was much harder. Mike and I had to gather the eggs, weed the garden, mow the grass, slop the hogs, round up the milk cows, milk the cows and work in the fields. Since I was inexperienced, I mainly just rode on the tractor. I wasn't very good at milking. It fact I don't think I ever learned to milk. It was a little frightening sometimes while gathering eggs from the chicken house. I started to reach into the nest for an egg one morning and saw a huge black snake there eating the egg. From that day forward I would look very closely before sticking my hand in the nest.

Before going out into the fields early in the mornings, we would put our drinking water in a gallon jug that was wrapped in a cloth bag to keep the water cool. Once I forgot my jug and one of the field hands offered me a drink out of his jug. After seeing the tobacco juice running down the side of his face, I decided I wasn't thirsty. Luckily there was a spring nearby that you could drink from. It seems hard to believe that the early pioneers drank from streams like these and even from the small creeks and rivers.

The best part of the day was at noon when I heard the dinner bell ring and on Friday night when we got cleaned up to go to town. All the farmers had a large cast iron bell mounted on a post near the house that was used to signal the farm hands that dinner was ready. You could easily hear the bell a couple of miles away and could tell by its loudness which farm it was coming from. At noon we would have a huge meal that had been prepared by the field hands wives. The farmers would trade out work with each other to get the crops in and the wives took care of preparing the food. I never saw so much food in my life. There was usually chicken, salt pork, roast beef several kinds of vegetables and various pies and cakes. I remember sometimes they would put a table cloth across the top of the food after dinner so it would be protected from the flies and ready for the next meal.

Most people only had a small ice box so food sitting out could spoil fairly quickly. Also the ice boxes weren't really that cold. However, I don't think people in those days ever thought about that. I always thought that an ice box kept foods cool with ice and a refrigerator kept foods cool with an electric compressor. However the old Wards catalogs called ice boxes refrigerators.

On Friday morning we would drag a wash tub full of cold well water out to the middle of the yard hoping that by evening the cold water would be warm. After being all day in the sun it still seemed to be cold to me. I also wanted to take my bath first. I didn't want to be second or third to use the same water. I guess that is where the old saying, "Don't throw the baby out with the bath water" came from. You would have thought that the baby would have gotten washed first before the water got so dirty.

My uncle Clyde would normally give Mike and me 50 cents to spend in Breckenridge on Friday night. There was one theatre that cost 15 cents and with a coke and popcorn at 5 cents we still had some money left over to buy candy or toys at the variety store. Sometimes there was a free movie shown in the park. It was usually sponsored by the local grocery store. I think it was called Places's Grocery. We would sit on a blanket in the grass and get eaten up by the mosquitoes.

The variety store had one 40 watt bulb in the center of the store so it was difficult to see much at night. We did buy black wax mustaches and orange wax whistles and red wax lips. We thought these to be really cool. After getting tired of them we would chew the wax until our mouths became so tired we had to spit it out. Also there were small wax bottles of colored liquid that tasted awful, but it was still fun to bite off the end and drink the liquid. Magic tricks and puzzles were also fun to buy at the variety store. The variety store was owned by my aunt Alice and Uncle Fritz Wolsey. We would then walk around the town square and harass the girls.

Almost every summer, I would break out in hives while visiting the farm where my cousin Mike and Aunt Winnie and Uncle Clyde lived. My Aunt would put salt and butter in a spoon and have me smear it over the itchy spots. It really felt good and actually stopped the itch. For some unknown reason, this made me hungry for corn on the cob.

The earliest house that my cousin Mike lived in had a small one room school house at the bottom of the hill. I thought it was strange to have each grade in separate rows and in the same room. This was quit different from my big city schools in St. Joe.

I tried to time my visits to coincide with the carnival that set up in the Breckenridge Park each spring. It was really exciting riding the Ferris wheel, tilt-a-whirl, bumper cars, and even the merry-go-round.

There were all types of games that if you were skillful enough you could win prizes. I later found out that most games were rigged in such a manner that it was almost impossible for you to win anything of value.

If you could throw a baseball and knock over a silver milk bottle you would win a giant teddy bear. The only problem was that the bottles were made out of metal with lead weights in the bottom making it very difficult to knock them over.

There was a claw machine that had lots of valuable prizes like watches at the bottom of the case but due to their size and weight it was easier to pick up the cheaper plastic toys and trinkets.

There was one game in which you could win prizes by spinning an arrow with a plastic pointer. If you were lucky it would stop on a valuable prize. The trouble was that the twisted metal stopper was turned in such a way that the pointer always slid by the expensive prizes and stopped on the cheap prizes. It was still a lot of fun trying and once in a while you would win a good prize. However, usually the prize was worth less than what it cost to play the game; especially if it took you several spins to win.

There were quite a few food booths featuring cotton candy, pop corn, snow cones, hot dogs and Coca Cola's or soda pop as we called it then.

It seemed as if everyone from miles around came to the carnival. It was an excellent place to meet some of your old friends and of course some pretty girls.

This is an earlier picture of Breckenridge's main street but in the 1940's it looked pretty much the same. The city park where the carnival was set up was directly west in the next block and on the south side of the street. I visited Breckenridge in 2007 and was very sad to see so many of the buildings gone. In the 1940's the old livery stable was still on the east side of town.

This is a picture of the park where the carnival would set up each year. This was my favorite time to vsit my cousin Mike.

My grandmother Wilson lived on a farm just North of Breckenridge. In the spring when they got heavy rains it was almost impossible to drive a car on her muddy road. I remember seeing my great granddad Weldon using his horses to pull out stuck automobiles. They didn't even have electricity or city water in the 1940's on the farm.

When it got dark Grandmother would light the kerosene lamps and great grandfather Joseph Weldon, Daddy Bill as he was called, would play the battery radio just long enough to hear the news. We would go to bed shortly after dark and get up at the crack of dawn. My grandmother would take me upstairs to bed carrying a kerosene lamp. Next to the bed was another kerosene lamp with a bowl of matches next to it. The bed had an itchy home made quilt and a feather bed mattress. There was a slop jar under the bed so if you had to go to the bathroom in the middle of the night you didn't have to go outside. That was very convenient but someone had to empty it the next morning.

It was really fun visiting my grandmother even though she didn't have all the comforts of city life. The thing I missed most on the farm was the indoor bathroom. The out house was on the other side of the chicken pen. The only side walks between the house and toilet was a narrow board laid on the ground. It kept you out of the mud but you had to step carefully as to not step on chicken crap. The outhouse was nice in that there were two holes. You didn't have to sit there alone. Doesn't seem too romantic but it was nice for us kids. I was always afraid of snakes and spiders and the mud dobbers (Wasps). It smelled awful so we always sprinkled lime into the hole and quickly covered it up with a wooden lid. There was seldom toilet paper. Instead you used the pages from an old Sears or Wards catalog or there was a bucket full of corn cobs. You didn't actually wipe with the corn cob. The cob was the handle and you wiped with the smooth husk. At least that was the way I did it. A favorite prank at Halloween was to push over a neighbors out house. Some times the owners would play their own prank by moving it themselves just before dark a few feet. The unexpecting prankster not being able to see well in the dark would then fall into the open pit.

The day trips to town were fun. At least we weren't working on the farm. The first stop was the Post Office off the main street in Breckenridge. I usually only stayed one or two weeks but looked forward to getting mail from mom. Mike and I were normally barefooted and the side walk was so hot in the summer time that we would run from the truck to the shops to keep from burning our feet.

We would sometimes deliver eggs to the poultry store and then pick up chicken feed at a feed store. Aunt Winnie would pick out some chicken feed that was in a sack suitable for making a shirt or dress. The last stop was usually the grocery store. The name of the store was "Places' Grocery" where sometimes we would trade milk, eggs and vegetables from the farm for other groceries. That's where the term "trading" came from. People today sometimes say that they trade at a particular store. Instead of actually trading they mean they just purchase things there.

Most of the old timers priced things in bits-same as the early colonists. I had a hard time getting used to that. A quarter was 2 bits, 4 bits was 50 cents, 6 bits was 75 cents, and 8 bits was a dollar. You rarely hear anyone using that terminology today.

In spite of all the work we had to do on the farm and a short memory, I was always ready to go back the next year.

My cousin, Mike Tomlin shared with me some information about Breckenridge during the early 1900's.. The main street of "Broadway" in Breckenridge was on what was called the "Ocean to Ocean highway" which was just a dirt road. There was a restaurant on the main street in Breckenridge called, "Pikes Peak Café."

The Pikes Peak Ocean to Ocean Highway (PPOO) was one of the early transcontinental highways in the U.S. (About 1910-1926). There was a meeting in St. Joseph, Missouri on March 18, 1914 to promote improvements and use of a road from New York City to San Francisco, California.

It followed mainly the old highway 36 and I believe went down Frederick Avenue to the river here in St. Joe and then on to Belleville, Kansas and on to California.

The Lure of the Open Road.

Good roads are made for Autos,
Autos are made to drive,
Come toot your horn—Don't be forlorn
Let's keep good roads alive.

The two lane highway 36 just south of Breckenridge replaced the old dirt road sometime in the 1930's. At the time of this writing, our present highway has been built a little further south of the old 36. I think they started working on that highway in the 1960's.

83

3,286 Mile Trip
(New York to California)

Concrete	664	miles
Bituminous macadam	486	"
Bituminous concrete	94	"
Brick	130	"
Gravel	1,242	"
Unsurfaced	670	"

Total: 3,286 miles

"On July 18, 1927, the highway association sponsored an Official Survey and Publicity Tour of the" PPOO" The tour was designed to direct nationwide attention to the highway, show how much time an average tourist would need to make the trip, and gather exact information on road mileage and condition. The official party included William L. Robinson of Mt. Vernon, Ohio, who was President of the association, and General Manager Judson. Robinson, because of an illness in his family, left the tour at Delaware, Ohio. However, at a banquet, he described the Pikes Peak Ocean to Ocean Highway as a long "Path of Friendship," with the towns along the way vying with their neighbors in entertaining and doing honor to the official party."

"The group left New York City on Monday morning, July 18, and reached Los Angeles on Thursday afternoon, August 11. Total driving time was 106 hours over 3,286 miles, which the official report of the tour noted is "the shortest route between New York City and Los Angeles." The trip averaged 31 miles an hour. The highway, the party found, was "continuously hard surfaced" from New York City to a

84

*point 50 miles west of Hannibal, Missouri (1,218 miles). Surface types, described as "hard surfaced road," encountered :...(Reference The Pikes Peak Ocean To Ocean Highway: The Appian Way of America **By Richard F. Weingroff)***

I can remember traveling from St. Joseph to Breckenridge in the 1940's on the old two lane 36 to visit my aunt, grandmother and cousin. We just barely made it one Christmas in the 1940's because the snow was so deep you could hardly see the road and had to drive by maneuvering in between the fence posts on each side of the road.

Larry Flinchpaugh riding cousin Mikes pony
"On second thought, maybe I was just sitting on it"

Larry's Uncle-Clyde Tomlin on left, unidentified man and cousin Mike and Aunt Winnie on right inside "Places Grocery Store" in Breckenridge where they did their "trading."

Breckenridge Produce Market Report
May 13, 1938

Hens...14 cents
Light Hens...............................11 cents
Springs.....................................17 cents
Leghorn Springs........................15 cents
Cream.......................................21 cents
Eggs.................................. ..18 cents

Note: The price of food has not gone up; the purchasing value of the dollar has gone down. In the 1950's you could buy 4 gallons of gas for a silver dollar. Today with silver at 18.00 per ounce, you can still buy 4 gallons of gas with a silver dollar but a paper dollar won't even buy one gallon. (This Hidden Inflation Tax is a well guarded secret and the favorite means for politicians to pay for their pork projects)

Chapter Eight
Newspaper Stories

Almost every month there was an article in the St. Joseph News Press featuring the reptile gardens and zoo. Occasionally, some of the stories appeared in other newspapers around the world. As described earlier there was the incident where Bill White was bitten by the cobra; also Vicky performing at the Krug Park Bowl.

At one time there was an incident that really had the postal employees upset at the post office on 8th street. My dad got a frantic call from the postal inspector advising him that a box of snakes that was being sorted for delivery to the reptile gardens had a hole in the box and there were several snakes loose in the post office.

My father rushed to the post office and spent about an hour rounding up all the snakes. Fortunately there were not any poisoness snakes in the bunch. The invoice showed that there were 20 snakes in the box but only 18 could be accounted for. When finished my dad told them that all had been found. I am sure they would have evacuated the entire post office if they had thought there were still some snakes running loose.

A short time later the United States Postal Service made it illegal to ship snakes through the mail. I am sure this incident had something to do with their ruling.

Vicky was in the news constantly. There was one time where she was featured on the front page of the paper having her haircut at "Hickman's" barber shop on Frederick

Avenue. There were several pictures of her in the barber shop in various poses. One was with her sitting in the barber chair with her head leaning backward with the caption, "once over lightly please." Another she was on top of the pay telephone with the caption, "Put one hand on me and I will call the cops." *(See pages 95-97)*

Sometimes the news stories would be picked up by the national news service which was the case of the heroic flight to save Bill Whites life as a result of him getting bitten by the cobra. In fact that story was in almost every major newspaper in the world.

One of Vicky's favorite places to go was 'Ozenbergers Ice Cream" shop on Frederick Avenue. She would sit up on the stool just like a regular customer.

Following are just some of the articles that appeared in the St. Joseph News Press:

St. Joseph News-Press
-1948-
Fondness for Pets
Leads St. Joseph Man Into Operation
of Shop for Their Sale

Parrots, Monkeys and Dogs Are Among His "Stock in Trade"

By JACK SUESENS
There is a lot of singing, playing, fighting, fussing, chattering and dancing going on at 603 South Eighth Street these days.

Occupants of the first floor rooms are rarely quiet. And even while the happy, vivacious ones are asleep and the more dour characters are maintaining dignified silence, they attract a great deal of attention.

Margery Flinchpaugh feeding the monkeys.

Indecision…The monkey would like some more of the milk and oatmeal he has smeared all over his face, but he is not too sure that reaching for it would lead to imprisonment. Apparently the gent in the cage is soured on the whole world, if the expression on his face be any indicator. Mrs. J. L. Flinchpaugh, wife of the proprietor of the Pet Shop, is doing the coaxing.

Collectively these inhabitants of 603 South 8th represent the hobby of a traveling salesman for a local wholesale grocer.

While most of them are native born, they represent, either personally or through their ancestors, the more exotic places in the world.

Unlike most men who, when absent, keep their pet projects under lock and key. J. L. Flinchpaugh leaves his in the capable hands of his wife.

Animals, Fish and Fowl

And Mr. Flinchpaugh"s hobby is a "pet" project in more than one sense of the word—it consists of owning and operating a pet shop.

According to Mrs. Flinchpaugh its anyone's guess as to whether the shop remains in operation for the sake of the customers or for the pleasure of her husband.

"Mr. Flinchpaugh always has been interested in animals," she explained yesterday. "This shop is his way of keeping close to them." Well, the shop's full of animals, all right. It's full of fish and fowl too.

Dogs in Top Rank

The big sales items are the dogs. As such they hold a place of honor in the front show window. At last inspection, the canine population included five-week-old fox terriers and eight-week-old wire-haired terriers and cocker spaniels.

Inside the doors of the pet shop, the inquisitive will find gold fish, tropical fish, monkeys, rabbits, flying squirrels, kittens, parrots, parakeets, cockatiels, canaries and snails. All the stuff that is to keep them in comfort is there too.

The monkeys are year old whiteface ringtails from Africa. One already is sold and is destined to be a Christmas present. Both have a weakness for milk and oatmeal.

Disdainful of the onlookers and, at times, quite vocal in contempt are the yellow head parrots at $100.00 each. A monkey brings $75.00.

Mrs. Flinchpaugh said yesterday that the shop dealt with all grades of dogs ranging from the common "pooch" to the aristocrat with papers.

Animals and birds are secured through regular distributors who sell pets to retailers in the same manner as others sell sacks of flour or cartons of cigarettes. Wholesalers mail out catalogs and price lists.

The Flinchpaugh"s adventures with animals were all the day's work right after they were married for they operated a "fur" farm five years at Kirksville. The couple moved to St. Joseph 15 years ago and opened their pet shop last June.

Note: With the Safeway store across the street and Ben Magoons Delicatessen, Einbenders, the drug store and the police station on 9th street, this area was fairly prosperous in the late 1940's.

It was an ideal location for a pet shop because the rent was much less than it would have been closer to the downtown area. The Safeway store manager saved all the day old bread and over ripened fruit for the monkeys'. It was close enough to downtown to walk to the many department stores and movie theatres.

-Time Line-

1932- Plainview Animal Farm in Kirksville, Missouri
1946-Opened Pet Shop at 8th and Messanie in St. Joe, Mo.
1951-Moved Pet Shop to 1202 Frederick Ave. St. Joe, Mo.
1954-Purchased the "Pony Express Reptile Gardens"
1963-Sold Reptile Garden property to the bank.
1963-Became director of "Weed Park Zoo" in Muscatine, Iowa.
1975- Returned to St. Joe to retire.

St. Joseph News-Press

Friday Evening, July 28, 1950

A Lion His Pet. . . Herman poses with his new owner, J. L. Flinchpaugh of the Flinchpaugh Pet Shop at 603 South 8th street. Herman a four-month old African black-maned lion, is the latest addition to the pet shop. Flinchpaugh received the "King of beasts" from the Al G. Kelly-Miller Brothers circus. The animal was shipped from Charlotte, Michigan where the circus was playing. Flinchpaugh indicated that the lion would be kept on display in the window of the pet shop until he gets too big. Then he will be sent to a zoo or circus. Herman has a diet of fresh horsemeat, milk with eggs in it, and cod liver oil.

St. Joseph News-Press
Sunday July 8, 1951

Local Pet Shop's
New Quarters
Now a Tourist Center

Tourists have discovered another attraction in St. Joseph—The Flinchpaugh Pet Shop. When the shop was moved to new quarters recently at 1202 Frederick Avenue it caught the highway 36 traffic and that on city route 71. At once a considerable number of travelers began to stop.

Puppies and birds are being purchased and taken off to both coasts. Some New Hampshire people walked into the store the other day and bought pets to be shipped back to their home. Then they bought others to send to friends or relatives in Arizona.

The Flinchpaugh store is a mass of movement. In one front window a couple of gila monsters slither about. Monkeys cavort in another window. Pups frisk about in boxes behind glass. Peruvian cavies are the rag mops of the store. They move by hops, making each one suddenly, as if from a hot spot. Kittens, birds, and tropical fish are in constant motion.

Flinchpaughs supplies a lot of tropical aquariums in St. Joseph. Tropicals are fascinating, but many varieties are hard to keep alive. Every fish fancier has trouble balancing an aquarium properly and keeping it clean. The Flinchpaugh tanks are kept spotless through the use of aerators and filters.

Beds, food, and supplies are stocked for pets. The store has a regular meat case filled with horse meat.

A very sad time for the Flinchpaugh family was when our first chimpanzee died. The News-Press covered the story as shown below.

St. Joseph News-Press

C. 1954

Baby Chimp Succumbs To Virus Pneumonia

A small, brightly painted room in the rear of Flinchpaugh"s Pet Shop where a pet chimpanzee lived and played will be empty today for the first time in three weeks. The chimp died early yesterday morning after a three day bout with virus pneumonia.

Attention was focused on the chimp two weeks ago when a picture of it and its owner, John L. Flinchpaugh, appeared in the News Press. Calls and personal messages flooded the pet shop congratulating the owner on his new "child."

Interest increased shortly after when Mr. Flinchpaugh ran a "name the Chimp" contest in which he offered the winner a free parakeet. Nearly a hundred persons visited the shop to suggest a name and to watch the antics of the four-and-a-half-month-old chimp.

"Everyone was interested in her," the owner said. "'I've never before seen an animal which could so completely win over the hearts of everyone who saw her.

"It was an awful blow for my wife and me," he said. Mr. Flinchpaugh said he first thought of giving the chimp a formal burial, "but I decided St. Joseph would benefit most if I gave it to the Museum." It's in the possession of Roy E. Coy, Museum curator, who will stuff and mount it.

𝔖t. 𝔍oseph 𝔑ews-𝔓ress

Sunday Morning July 17, 1955

Here's What the Barber Went Through to Give Vicki a Haircut

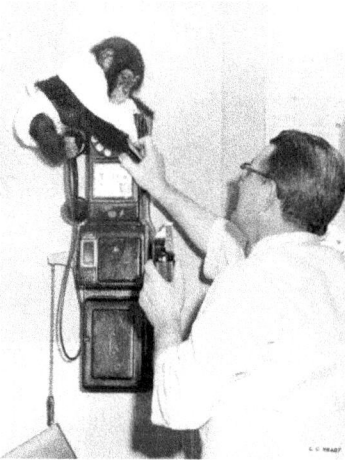

"Lay a finger on me and
I will have the cops here
in 5 minutes."

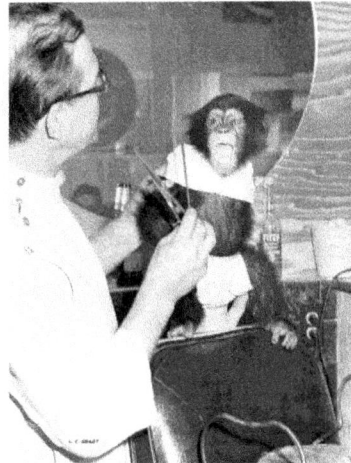

"Hey, put those scissors
away. What is this? A clip
Joint!"

Note: Vicky Lynn didn't actually ever get haircuts. She was real-ly a good sport when these pictures were taken. This was the talk of the town for several months after they appeared in the News Press. The publicity that the News Press did with Vicky was largely responsible for her popularity.

Even today, 2010, people stop me on the street and want to know whatever happened to Vicky. Literally thousands of people re-member reading about her in the paper, seeing her perform at the zoo and the Krug Park Bowl and seeing her on KFEQ T.V.

"I don't know that I want my hair cut. I'm
already pretty enough."

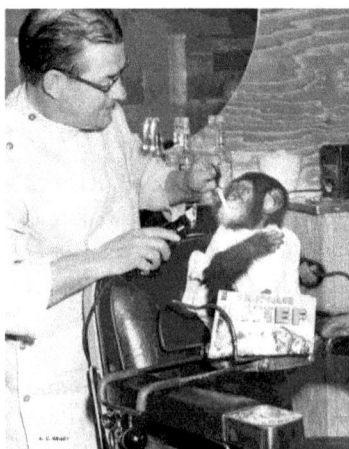

"Thanks for the cigarette.
This isn't going to be as bad
as I thought."

"Okay, I'll sit back down.
But no monkey business
Mr. Barber."

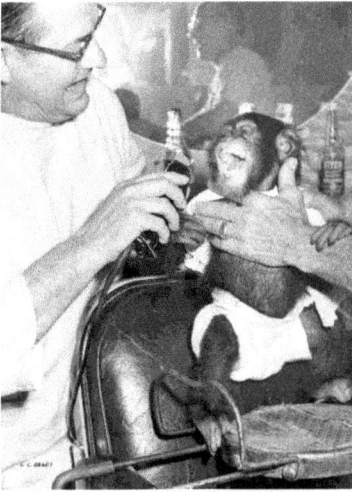

"Hey, wait a minute, that
stuff's smelly. Lemme
Outa here."

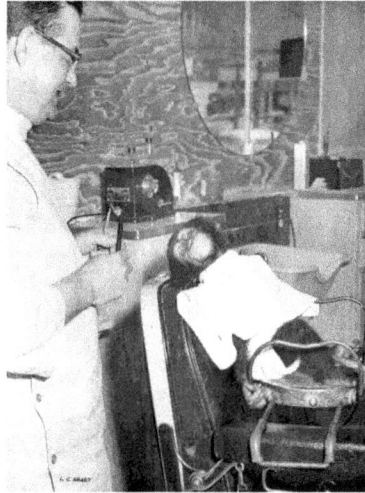

"A barber chair is sure relaxing.
Once over lightly please."

These photos were taken at Hickman's Barber Shop on Frederick Avenue by News Press photographer L. C. Shady.

Vicky enjoyed getting away from the zoo and having new experiences like visiting the barber shop or going to Osenberger's on Frederick for ice cream.

One cold winter day, my mother had wrapped Vicky up completely, because of the extreme cold, to take her from the car to the photographer in downtown St. Joe. One of my mother's friends saw her and thought she must be carrying her new granddaughter. My mother's friend, wanting to see the new baby, pulled back the blanket and was startled to see Vicky instead of a human baby.

Like humans, Vicky was very susceptible to getting colds and even pneumonia.

97

Independence Daily News

Wednesday August 15, 1956

Five Cents per Copy

HERKIMER IS HERE AT LAST

HERKIMER IS HERE AT LAST—An estimated four hundred curious spectators turned out at the Independence Hospital to welcome him. Herk, who after all, turned out to be a friendly chimpanzee, is seen here being led by trainer, J. L. Flinchpaugh. He is dressed in a surgical gown.
(Daily News Photo)

Band Music, Photographers and Large Crowd Greets Dr. Herkimer

About 2,000 people were on hand at the Independence Sanitarium and Hospital parking lot west of the hospital to greet Dr. Herkimer. Dr. Herkimer, who turned out to be a lovable chimpanzee, greeting the curious crowd with a toothy smile and clung to his trainer J. L. Flinchpaugh, all the tighter.

The arrival which was set for 11:15 this morning was delayed slightly and finally the crowd was rewarded with, sight of the helicopter about 11:30. The copter circled the parking lot once and then made a general swing over town. On the swing, leaflets were dropped urging people to give to the hospital fund.

The doctor finally landed and he was immediately swamped with hand shakers and young children. "Herk", as almost everyone in town calls him by now was a bit set back by the battery of photographers and newsreel camera men. Photographers and reporters from every major news service in the country were present and the flash of cameras and the whir of moving news reel cameras predominated. John Newhouse, city attorney was the official and he was the first to shake hands with the doctor. Herkimer was dressed in a white surgical gown but other than this he was unclad.

Radio station KCMO had Bob Strack on the scene making a personal interview with dignataries but Bob could not get a word out of "Herk." Phil Turner had a brass band on hand to provide the music for the gala affair.

After shacking many hundred hands and smiling for about as many pictures Herkimer tried his hand at leading the band. He got them going but gave up when the music got to loud.

The doctor was then wisked off in a new convertible to the Square where he was officially greeted by Mayor Bob Weatherford. More hand shaking and more pictures followed and from there he went to a Chamber of Commerce dinner. He has a very full agenda for the day with dinners, visits and other semi-official duties. He will visit the police

99

station and assume the duties of police sometime tomorrow.

Omaha World Herald
December 8, 1956.

Vickie Lynn and teacher . . . basket ball next?

Chimp Mastering Skates;
Basket Ball Next on List?
The World-Herald's News Service

St. Joseph, Mo.---Most folks, when they think of Sidney,
Iowa recall the rodeo which is an annual highlight of the
Southwest Iowa town.

But here in the northwest corner of Missouri whenever
Sidney is mentioned , folks associate it with Norma Lee
Johnston.

Mrs Johnston is the daughter of Mr. And Mrs. L. L.
Blackburn of Sidney. She and her husband, Carl, operate
the Skateland Roller rink here.

100

Two years ago Norma Lee, who formerly played basket ball with Omaha Commercial Extension, was named to the Women's National AAU All-America team while competing for the St. Joseph, Goetz club.

Now Norma Lee is making headlines again—this time as a roller skating instructor with a most unusual pupil, a chimpanzee.

Vicky Lynn, 2, is the star student, roller skating is the latest of her achievements which include eating with a knife and fork, brushing her teeth and sipping liquids through a straw.

Mrs Johnston says Vicky Lynn, who belongs to Mr. and Mrs. John Flinchpaugh, owners of the reptile gardens here, is learning faster than the average child.

Vickie's natural sense of balance accounts for her quick learning.   When Vicky Lynn has mastered the art of roller skating, what next?   "Well," comments Mrs. Johnston, "there's always basket ball."

Photo by L.C. Shady-News Press

101

St. Joseph now has a sea lion. Shown above is Toby, a two year old Pacific Coast specimen who was flown here this week from his previous home in Phoenix. He is now in the Flinchpaugh exhibition. He is gentle and frolicsome and weighs about 100 pounds. He has had no training as yet but seems to have the temperament to be taught many tricks.

Postal Nerves Shaken by Loose Snake in Mail Sack

By ROBERT L. SLATER

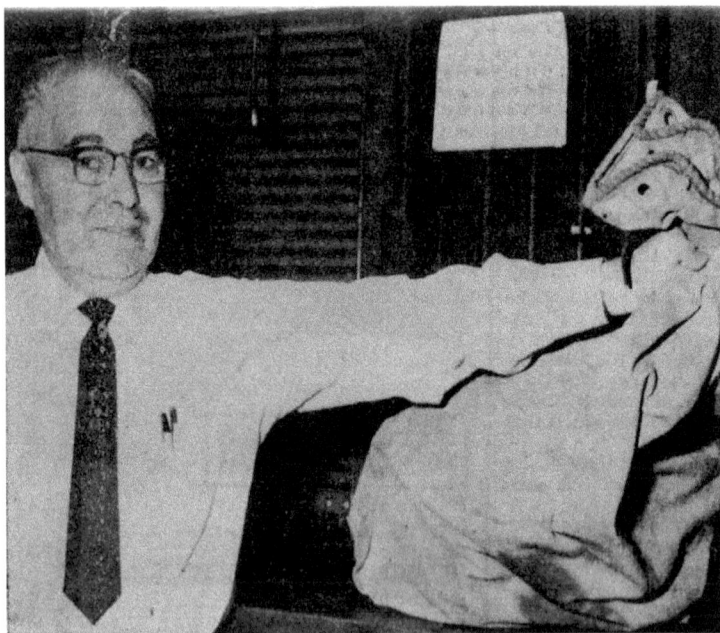

Leo H. Seckles, superintendent of mails, is about as close to the sack of snakes as anyone got this morning before the arrival of J. L. Flinchpaugh a reptile expert.

A large canvas mail sack addressed to the St. Joseph postmaster arrived here this morning, but Theo J. Quinn didn't open it.

Neither did any other postal employee.

In addition to the address, the cardboard label attached to the mail bag also carried the notation, "Live snakes loose in sacks." The sack was tightly closed at the neck, and fastened with a lock

Postal officials summoned J. L. Flinchpaugh, operator of a reptile garden here, for assistance. Awaiting his arrival, a large number of postal workers came close enough to the mail bag to get a good look at it, but none made any effort to unfasten the lock and peek inside.

Quinn Plays Safe

It was shortly after 10 when Mr. Flinchpaugh arrived in the office of Leo H. Seckles, superintendent of mails. The mail bag was brought to that room by S. D. Alexander, assistant superintendent of mails.

While Postmaster Quinn and about 40 of the postal workers looked on from a safe distance, Mr. Flinchpaugh reached in the sack. The first item pulled out was a snake about 30 inches in length.

"Perfectly harmless," said Mr. Flinchpaugh. He let the snake bite his finger just to prove the point. The postal people still weren't completely convinced. None offered to stick their own fingers in the snake's mouth.

Also Some Toads

That turned out to be the only loose snake in the bag. The others, about half a dozen in all, were wrapped in separate cloth sacks. One of the sacks contained some toads, incidentally. The loose snakes had escaped through a hole in their cloth sack, and then worked their way out of a cardboard box which contained the sacks. It was when that box came open and the snakes peered forth, apparently, that the entire shipment had been placed in the canvas sack.

The loose snake was described by Mr. Flinchpaugh as a King snake. Others in the shipment were hognoses and chicken snakes, he said.

The cardboard box indicated the snakes had been shipped from Wilmington, North Carolina and were intended for Mr. Flinchpaugh. Postal officials who summoned the reptile man here did not know they were intended for him at that time, since the tag on the canvas sack contained no such information. The tag did indicate the cardboard box and its contents had been transferred to the canvas sack at Fulton, Kentucky.

A Snake Exchanger

Mr. Flinchpaugh says he frequently exchanges snakes and other animals with the operator of a reptile garden there. He was not aware the shipment was coming.

Postal regulations permit mailing snakes, with the approval of the postmaster-general, Mr. Seckles said. The cardboard box was properly marked, indicating its contents, and there was no violation of post office regulations.

St. Joseph News-Press
Monday, Feb. 1, 1960

Circus Troup Presents Show At Flinchpaughs

St. Joseph's new circus attraction was so well received yesterday that its stay may be prolonged for several weeks. A large crowd saw the first performance Sunday at Flinchpaugh"s Pet Shop and Reptile Gardens on highway 36, just east of the Belt highway. "We will have the show again next Sunday," J. L. Flinchpaugh said today. "We will have it each Sunday, as long as the circus folks are here. That may be up to spring."

In the troup are Mr. And Mrs. Dale Madden Sr., Lake City, Iowa; their son, Dale Madden Jr. and his wife, and Al Szasz, all circus people.

Awaiting Summer Season

Friends of the Flinchpaugh"s, they came to St. Joseph while waiting for the summer circus season to open. A part of the troupe arrived two months ago and the rest two weeks ago.

With the Reptile Gardens as headquarters the troup has been busy performing for schools and clubs in the St. Joseph area.

Yesterdays show lasted about 40 minutes. Its music was provided by Dale Madden Sr. at the organ and his son, drummer and organist.

Trained Dogs, Monkeys

The acts included trained dogs and monkeys, whip cracking and a wrestling match between Al Szasz and Victor, a big Canadian black bear.

At the end, Vicky, the Flinchpaugh"s chimpanzee rode on different size bicycles and performed other tricks.

Mt. Flinchpaugh said the acts probably will vary from week to week as other circus friends drop in.

𝔖t. 𝔍oseph 𝔑ews-𝔓ress

July 16, 1961

Chimp Aids Harvard Prof

Vicki Lynn, Teacher Appear in Film to Make Biology More Attractive to Students

By ROBERT L. SLATER

Photograph by Calvin Productions-Kansas City, Mo.

Vicki Lynn will help teach biology to high school students. Now Vicki Lynn isn't exactly a teacher. In fact she's a six year old, 70 pound chimpanzee, the property of John L. Flinchpaugh.

But Vicki Lynn and a Harvard professor have collaborated in an effort to make biology more attractive for high school students. Admittedly, the Harvard professor did the talking, all of it. But Vicki Lynn played a major role in the effort to make biology more attractive and easy to understand.

30- Minute Movie

For eight hours—with time out only for lunch—she stood before movie cameras a few days ago while Dr. G. E. Erikson talked. Doctor Erikson, shown above with Vicki Lynn, is assistant professor of anatomy at Harvard Medical School.

The finished product, according to Mr. Flinchpaugh, will be a 30-minute movie, devoted to a study of the chimpanzee's features and habits.

The filming took place at Kansas City. The movie will be part of a 120-film series on biological subjects. The program is sponsored by the American Institute of Biological Sciences, and supported by the National Science Foundation and the Atomic Energy Commission.

A Chauffeur Role

Mr. Flinchpaugh doesn't appear in the movie himself. He merely drove Vicki Lynn to Kansas City. He's had the chimpanzee since she was a few months old, and has trained her to perform a variety of acts. Vicki Lynn has appeared at a number of public events in this area, including one trip to Lincoln, Nebraska.

Mr. Flinchpaugh, who operates a zoo and reptile gardens here, said the persons making the film inquired about other animals which he has available. It is possible some of the other animals or some reptiles will be used in other films in the series, he said.

The completed film series will be offered to high schools through-out the nation, Mr. Flinchpaugh was told.

The films are being produced by Calvin Productions, Inc.,
Kansas City, for the McGraw-Hill Book Co. The film series will represent a complete high school biology course.

St. Joseph News-Press
Monday, June 5, 1961

A LOT OF SNAKE

Photograph by Bill Bennett-St. Joseph Gazette

It took seven husky men to hold this 18-foot snake, which
arrived yesterday at Flinchpaugh"s Pet Shop and Reptile
Garden at 3727 Frederick Boulevard and even they couldn't
straighten the water boa to its full length. The huge reptile,
called an Anaconda, is native to South America and was
received here through the Miami, Florida Serpentarium.
After getting its picture snapped, the snake was put in a
cage at the gardens for display.

Holding the Anaconda are (from left to right) Art Wilson,
Carl Johnston, Leroy Powell, Steve Reynolds, Don Neu-

man, Dr. Charles Deming, veterinarian, and John Flinch-paugh owner of the reptile Gardens.

Dr. Deming's veterinarian hospital was next to the Reptile Gardens and Carl Johnston owned the skating rink just west of the Belt and Frederick.

The New York Times
Wednesday, July 26, 1961

Lion adorns Flinchpaugh's Zoo at St .Joseph, Mo.

Native folk art, which was mourned as dead, is apparently still alive, an art institute has discovered in travels around the country. Native and vigorous, like their earlier counterparts, primitive art works were found on roadside stands, zoos, a miniature golf course, shoe repair shops, and other small commercial establishments from Florida to New England and on roads from the East to Pacific coasts. The discoverer is Mrs. Nina Howell Starr....

Flinchpaugh"s zoo in St. Joseph, Missouri has both the real thing and painted representations of lions and alligators.

True Davis, president of Philips-Roxane, while on a business trip to New York City mailed this article to my father. A traveling artist had painted several pictures of lions, alligator, lizards, etc on the side of the building as a means to attract attention to passer bys.

St. Joseph News-Press
March 23, 1962

Captain William (Bill) Forbes giving Vicky a speeding ticket

Vicki Lynn, chimpanzee owned by John Flinchpaugh, gives her owner a perplexed look as Police Lieutenant William Forbs prepares to issue a ticket to the bicycle-riding animal. Its all in fun and the picture was posed yesterday to call attention to the police department's bicycle clinic.

Vicki will give an exhibition of safe bicycle riding during the clinic April 7 at the police court room. Vicki went along with the picture, then promptly proved to several persons that she is a safe bicycle rider as she peddled around the parking lot at Flinchpaugh's Pet Shop on highway 36.

Talented Chimp on Program at Clinic For Bicycle Riders

The St. Joseph police department's bicycle clinic April 7 promises to be entertaining as well as instructional.

Vicki Lynn, talented chimpanzee at the Flinchpaugh Reptile Garden, will appear on the clinic program in an exhibition of proper bicycle riding.

"Monkeying around on a bicycle is serious business and we hope by using the chimp we can impress on the youngsters the safety factors involved in careful bicycling" said Traffic Lieut. Bill Forbes who will preside over the clinic.

Vicki, who can skillfully ride any size bicycle, will be handled by her owner and trainer, John Flinchpaugh.

The newspaper article continues on about the facts and necessity of the upcoming bicycle clinic sponsored by the Police Department.

St. Joseph News-Press

Tuesday Evening, June 12, 1962

St. Joseph's Bambi Has a Son

Bambi had no objection when the photographer wanted to get a picture of her fawn, born Sunday, but she wanted to let the whole world know she was mighty pride of the baby and gave it a motherly kiss as the picture was snapped. Holding the fawn is Mrs. John Flinchpaugh. The baby is a six pound boy. Bambi and son are members of the Flinch-paugh animal collection on Frederick avenue east of the belt.

112

Sunday Times-Democrat
Davenport – Bettendorf, Iowa
April 28, 1963

Muscatine's new superentendent of Weed Park Zoo and
Vicky, trained chompanzee. (Staff photos)

A Great Life
With His Wild
Animal Pals

By STAFF WRITER

MUSCATINE, Iowa—"You don't have to be plain dunb to mess around with animals –but it helps," grinned John Flinchpaugh, new superintendent of this city's Weed Park Zoo.

It's soon evident it's not "dumbness," but a knowledge of animals gained from long experience and a genuine love for any wild thing which makes the wiry Flinchpaugh a natural for the job.

"If money was the only thing there'd never be a zoo keeper, but if you love animals it's a real pleasure to have your work and your hobby all tangled together. "But it would be terrible for someone who didn't enjoy working with animals. They couldn't do it. It would drive them crazy, all the trouble they have to absorb. An animal man has to have, above all, patience—lots and lots of patience," Flinchpaugh stressed.

Personality Profile

His experience with wild creatures dates back to 1926 when he operated a wild animal farm in Kirksville, Missouri. For the past 17 years, Flinchpaugh has operated a reptile gardens, zoo and pet shop in St. Joseph, Mo.

He is very enthusiastic about the Weed Park Zoo. "Why, for a town and area of this size it's a wonderful zoo. The people are lucky to have such a fine one—and a free one, at that!"

Flinchpaugh didn't come empty handed, either. He brought with him the animals and reptiles from his animal farm in Missouri. The zoos reptile house is now stocked with a ball python, a rock python, a 15 foot red-tailed boa constrictor, and a baby boa which turned up in St. Joseph in a bunch of bananas.

114

His contribution also includes, in addition to various other snakes and reptiles, an ocelot, puma, llama, a rare snowy owl, and a most talented young lady, Vicky Lynn a trained chimpanzee. Asked about Vicky's accomplishments, Flinchpaugh replied modestly, "Aw I kind of hate to say all she can do. I sound like a parent bragging about his kid. However..."**the 8 year old chimp can ride a bike, hula dance, walk on high stilts, play the drum, do flip-flops, stand on her head, put a dime in a pop machine and drink the pop from the bottle when it comes out, walk a wire, roll a bbbarrel, waltz, brush her teeth—yes and roller skate.**

Vicky is even a "movie star." "recently a professor from Harvard university made a 30-minute movie of Vicky. It was for a social science series on primates. It is to be shown in high schools, " Flinchpaugh explained.

"That was tough, "he admitted. "Vicky is reaching the age where she is a little bit crochety. It took about eight hours to shoot the movie and they wanted her to keep still for long periods of time.

A Friendly Kiss

She was getting pretty fidgety and I couldn't keep the chain on her while they were taking the pictures. I sat there with a gun in one hand (*loaded with blanks*) and a piece of candy in the other, just hoping she wouldn't take a chunk out of anyone." Vicky is deathly afraid of the gun and bends her head and covers her face with her hands when Flinchpaugh displays it.

She frequently gives her boss a friendly kiss and at times deftly unbuttons his shirt.

"You get to know a lot about animals' moods when you have been around them a lot. You learn how they react. Don't think they don't know instantly if you are afraid of them. They are much more apt to attack if they know you are afraid of them."

Flinchpaugh, who began his duties March 1, is currently in the process of getting acquainted with the zoo's animals.

"They have to get to know and trust you and you have to get to know them. For instance, I'm just getting used to "Candy" the elephant. I don't know what cues she's used to so I'm kind of feeling my way. I can make her lift her foot or sit down now. Eventually I'll be able to lead her all over the park, but I wouldn't try it now. Not until she gets better acquainted with me."

Flinchpaugh donned heavy leather gloves to display a fiercely snarling ocelot about three feet long. It kept sinking its teeth and sharp claws into his gloves and tried to bite through his overshoes.

When Flinchpaugh withdrew the gloves, he had two ugly, bleeding scratches on his hand. He just smiled, "One of the hazards of the business."

It's true. An elephant did fall on John Flinchpaugh and broke his ankle.

Muscatine Zoo Gets A New Baby Elephant And Her Keeper Gets A Broken Ankle.

116

New Baby For The Zoo
By JIM ARPY

MUSCATINE Iowa--Muscatine zoo director John Flinchpaugh sits down as he pats Dolly, the zoo's new elephant. Flinchpaugh is on crutches from an injury incurred when Dolly fell on him.

When people see John Flinchpaugh hobbling around with his broken left ankle in a cast and ask what happened, he says straighted faced that an elephant fell on him, and they laugh and say, "Oh, boy an elephant, that's a good one!"

The only thing is that Flinchpaugh, director of this city's Weed Park Zoo isn't kidding. An elephant really did fall on him.

Fortunately it wasn't a big elephant as elephants go. In fact, it was 'Dolly", a new addition to the zoo, and just a baby weighing a meer 700 pounds.

Flinchpaugh and an assistant were training two year old "Dolly" to lie down. Her feet were trussed up with ropes and both men were pulling mightly to get the elephant in the prone position.

Suddenly Flinchpaugh's feet slipped on the wet concrete in the elephant pen and he fell down. At that very moment Dolly tumbled over, landing on the zoo keepers left leg, breaking the ankle.

117

I'm probably the only guy around who's had an elephant fall on him," Flinchpaugh grins. He went right back to work the next day, and is still getting around on crutches.

Dolly, a little gal with lots of personality, was obtained from a Burlington, Wisconsin animal dealer, replacing the zoo's elephant, "Candy" whose bulk was rapidly becoming too much for her pen.

Candy didn't take kindly to her replacement and treated Dolly quite roughly when the two were put in together, Flinchpauh says. Candy was sold to a Rock Falls man.

Dolly (named after "Hello Dolly") hails originally from Thailand. Customarily African elephants have two small "fingers" at the tips of their trunks, while Asian elephants like Dolly have just one.

She's an exception, because her trunk has two fingers— just like those of her African counterparts. Though Flinchpaugh has been training her for only a few weeks , Dolly has proven herself an apt pupil.

Nimbly she leaps up on a tub, stands on two feet, and lifts her trunk high over her head upon command. She has gained about 100 pounds since her arrival a few weeks ago.

Obviously much attached to her new master, Dolly follows Flinchpaugh about like a dog. She likes to have her back scratched with a broom, and is still fuzzy with long "baby hair."

Flinchpaugh says the free zoo now boasts 165 specimens of birds, animals and reptiles. Newest addition to the zoo is a buffalo calf, born to parents confined to the park.

Article in the Muscatine, Iowa paper

October 6, 1970

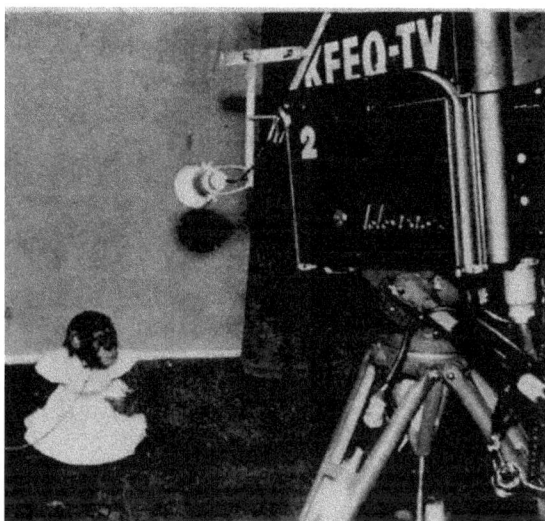

Vicky became very much in demand as an entertainer after several appearances on Zoo Day, a weekly television program in St. Joseph Missouri. Vicky was a regular feature for five years. She played the part of a celebrity very well. She dined in restaurants, flew by helicopter, and airplane and was featured in the newspaper on many occasions. Mr Flinchpaugh has a scrapbook with many articles and photographs of her career.

Vicky's most important fete, perhaps was her part in helping raise $300,000 for a new hospital. (*Independence, Missouri*)

In 1961, she stood for eight hours before movie cameras for the Harvard Medical School with Dr. G. E. Erickson, professor of anatomy. The film was thirty minutes in length when finished, and was used all over the United States in high school biology departments.

When the Flinchpaugh's came to Muscatine, Vicky was still making public appearances, her last was a circus day promotion in Davenport, in 1963. She was not on her best behavior that day, and Mr. Flinchpaugh decided it should be her last appearance. He says it is their nature to become a little dangerous as they get older, particulary if they get annoyed with someone in the crowd.

Vicky followed the Flinchpaugh's to Niabi Zoo in Rock Island County where she met her true love, "Junior". However they were separated when Vicky came back to Weed Park Zoo in Muscatine. This story does conclude happily, because this summer, "Junior" came to Muscatine to make his home with Vicky. When he arrived they hugged and kissed and held hands. It is hoped that this love affair will produce a Vicky Lynn the 2nd, to entertain the children of Muscatine.

The next time you visit Weed Park Zoo, be sure to pay your respects to Vickie Lynn—Celebrity—Chimpanzee

---

Epilog

Looking Back At
A More Prosperous Time

I hope that you have enjoyed our journey exploring life in the 1940's through the 1960's in St. Joe and reading about the various animal stories relating to my father's pet shop, reptile gardens and zoo. St. Joe was and still is a wonderful place to grow up. Our boulevard and park system is probably as beautiful as any in the world. The small town atmosphere and the friendliness of the people are by far superior to life in the big cities. I know many of you visited the zoo when you were children and have fond memories of personally interacting with all the many varieties of animals and seeing Vicky Lynn perform not only on TV but in person. All the animals, but in particular Vicky, were definitely a large part of my life and gave me a solid foundation on which to build my life as an adult.

Oddly enough, the only pet I have now is a wild raccoon that comes to my door every night looking for food. I first met her when she was caught peeking through our kitchen's glass sliding door. She was so cute I just couldn't resist her plea for something to eat. As time progressed she would return several times each night for more food. I finally figured out that there were actually **three** raccoons coming each night. You know they all wear a mask and it is difficult to tell them apart. I call our favorite one "Bandit" and my wife Phyllis calls her "Miss America" because she always says, "here she comes- Miss America."

As you read the stories and view the old post cards of St. Joe in the early days, one wonders if St. Joe and towns like Breckenridge were more prosperous and economically stable in the past. We had more industries than today providing job opportunities and economic strength for our community. We have seen the closure of many businesses like Swifts, Armours, Quaker Oats, Western Tablet Factory, Noma Lights, etc. I guess you could say the same is true for many other small communities as well that have experienced hard economic times.

What happened? It has been written by other writers that St. Joe just never was the same after the great depression of the 1930's followed by the devastating WW ll and the resulting enormous debt accrued to the American people. I would like to mention some other reasons which would also apply to the country in general.

Following the war, the great interstate highway system was developed which encouraged the population to migrate away from the city center with the businesses soon following. The big box stores soon came in, locating near the highways and the new suburban population. Many of the smaller stores could simply not adapt to the changes being made. Not only did we lose many of our small businesses but later we lost many of our larger ones with their migration to other countries. Literally millions of our good manufacturing jobs were lost due to unfair trade agreements like NAFTA. But this is just part of the story. What else happened? It is almost like the answer to this question is a big secret. You rarely hear it being discussed on the nightly news or in the newspapers.

What am I talking about? There were three major changes in this country's economic system beginning in the first part of the 20th century- two in 1913 and the other starting in the 1920's that few people understand but which have affected us more than any other events. It is not in the scope of this book to go into a great amount of detail on this subject but I will briefly discuss these three issues that are in my opinion, causing most of our economic problems today.

These three issues are the most important ones you will ever come in contact with in your entire life. Of course this is just my belief but I hope I can prove it to you and encourage you to do further research in this area so you can be a part of the process to save our country from financial ruin.

The three events that have affected us the most are (1) the passing of the Federal Reserve Act in 1913 authorizing a **private** bank to be in control of our country's monetary system, (2) the adoption of the 16th Amendment also in 1913 making it possible for the Federal Government to collect an income tax on its citizen's wages, and (3) the destroying of the small family farms not only in America but the entire world by replacing them with large corporate factory farms (Agribusiness).

Most people believe that the Federal Reserve is a department of the Federal Government. <u>It is not</u>. It is listed in the white pages of the phone book next to Federal Express. It is a privately owned banking cartel in existence to make a profit by issuing and controlling our country's money supply, a profit in which we citizens do not share.

When our government needs money, it either raises taxes or it borrows it from the privately owned Federal Reserve and creates a bond payable to the Federal Reserve. Incredibly, the Fed charges us interest for loaning us our own money! Our Treasury Department simply prints the paper money as a service to the **private** Federal Reserve. The truth is that the U.S. Constitution allows the Federal Government to print its own money, <u>interest free</u>. Why in the world should we entrust this important function to a private bank that charges us unnecessary interest?

Presidential candidate William Jennings Bryan in his famous "Cross of Gold" speech in 1895, said**…"Those who are opposed to this proposition tell us that the issue of paper money is a function of the bank and the government ought to go out of the banking business. I stand with Jefferson rather than with them, and tell them as he did, that the issue of money is a function of the government and that the banks should go out of the governing business..."**

 If the Fed was abolished and we stopped being the policeman of the world, an income tax on our wages would be absolutely unnecessary. A study a few years ago showed that most taxes collected by the IRS on peoples' salaries do not go to pay for services for the people at all but rather pays mainly for the interest the privately run Federal Reserve charges the American public for printing and loaning us our own money. People will usually say, "how will we pay for our schools and highways?' Easy! Schools are paid for by county property taxes and highways by the motor fuel tax you pay when you fill up your auto with gas.

Just think what kind of stimulus this would be to you as an individual and also to the economy of St. Joe and other communities if you were not required to pay income tax on your salary. All of a sudden we would have enough money for municipal projects; fix our sewer system, and improve the streets, curbs, sidewalks, parks, etc. Plus there would be almost full employment due to the more healthy economy.

The IRS would not need to be eliminated as the fear- mongers suggest. They would still be needed to handle the legitimate taxes collected on corporate and small business profits and profits on capital gains of stocks, bonds and commercial real-estate.

An income tax on your wages is not only unconstitutional but is a form of slavery. You actually work a portion of each day for free just to pay the tax. Isn't it a form of slavery when you are required to work and not get paid for it? All you are doing is trading your labor and sweat for money. Where is the profit in that? Why should that be taxable?

The Federal government should be protecting the value of our dollar. Shouldn't we be able to put a dollar bill under our mattress today and twenty years later pull it out and still be able to purchase the same amount of goods and services? When I was a kid, a gallon of gas cost 25 cents and a silver dollar would buy four gallons. Today a silver dollar is worth about 18.00 and will still buy 4 gallons of gas with a little left over but a paper dollar won't even buy one gallon. Does that tell you what has happened to the purchasing power of the paper dollar? Ask yourself, "Has the cost of goods and services gone up or has the purchasing power of your paper dollar gone down?"

And the third event that affects us is the farm issue. Starting in the 1920's, the Rockefeller Foundation, the Ford Foundation, Monsanto, and the USDA set out to destroy the small family farms worldwide and replace them with large corporate farms (Agribusiness). Their <u>public</u> agenda was to conquer world hunger by developing "Genetically Modified seeds" and other programs that would yield much higher food production per acre. However, their <u>private</u> or <u>secret</u> agenda was to capture the entire world's food producing business and control population growth. Many of these genetically altered crops reduce fertility rates and affect our health. We still have world hunger and the small farms that have been destroyed have severely reduced the living standard of much of the world.

Only an informed electorate can pressure their representatives to return our country to that which was envisioned by our founding fathers. Start now by studying the important issues facing us today and begin electing those representatives who will have our government (1) abide by the Constitution, (2) abolish the private Federal Reserve Banking system, (3) stop being the policeman of the world, (4) recognize the sovereignty of the individual states and (5) support programs that will help reestablish the small family farms.

For more information regarding these issues, I would like to recommend that you read my book that I published in May, 2009 entitled, "*Secrets of Our Hidden Controllers Revealed.*" Also I have reprinted a pamphlet, with my comments, called "*Billions for The Bankers--Debts For the People*" *which explains the evils of our current banking system.*

After retiring, I have been studying the important issues that affect all of us, and have discovered that many of our opinions about these most important issues are in error. Many of our government leaders, the controlled mainstream media, our educational system, and even our religious organizations have kept us from learning the truth.

Some who have read my book, **"Secrets of Our Hidden Controllers Revealed"** and my numerous letters to the editor, claim that my views are "revolutionary" and outside the mainstream? To discredit me and those like me in the various Tea Party groups and other political activist groups, we are unfairly labeled as unpatriotic, racists, "Conspiracy Nuts", Anti-Semitic", Paranoid", "Radicals", "Birthers", "Tax Protesters", etc.

Just who are the real patriots anyway? Should you be considered a patriot simply because you salute the flag and wear a flag lapel pen? In my opinion, the majority of our elected leaders are certainly not patriots. They don't honor the oath they swore to uphold and think the constitution is outdated. Never mind that our founding fathers wrote the constitution considering human nature. Human nature of acquiring power and wealth has not changed. I would say that there is a higher percentage of true patriots involved in organizations like **Campaign for Liberty** the **Tea Party** groups, **Oath Keepers** and the **John Birch Society** than in our government and the national news media.

By today's standards of the controlling elite and the dummed down electorate, George Washington, Thomas Jefferson and Benjamin Franklin would be labeled as unpatriotic or possible terrorists or militia members.

Be wary of those labeling the political activist groups un-fairly. It just may be that those doing the labeling are the **unpatriotic** ones and the people they are attempting to marginalize are the **true patriots**.

Remember there are three types of people. Those that make things happen, those that watch things happen and those that just sit back and say **"What happened?"**

Which one of these people do you want to be?

Photo Gallery and Time Line

Flinchpaugh ZOO
Opening for the Summer
Sunday, June 4th

Lion, big and little Monkeys, Wild Boar, Bears, Martin, Acconti-Mundi, Ring Tail Cats, 145-lb. Baboon, Chinese Dragons, Leopards, and others.

Bigger and Better! Admission Only 10c
OR ONE FREE ADMISSION
With every purchase of 5 gallons of

POWERFUL! PANKEY Swan
HI-TEST
GASOLINE

It Is Lubricated and At No Extra Cost
You will marvel at the performance of your motor
—SMOOTH AND POWERFUL—
JOHNNIE FLINCHPAUGH ZOO–SOUTH OF KIRKSVILLE
On Highway 63 at the Junction with Highway 6

Plainview Wild Animal Farm and "Silver Fox Service Station
Kirksville, Missouri (1932)
The ads promoting his zoo advertised as having 350 animals on display. One cold winter one of his monkeys gave birth in the frigid cold, so the baby was aptly named, "Zero." These were hard times during the depression making it necessary for my fa ther to once again take a salesman's job with "Western Grocery Company" temporarily taking him out of the animal business.

Announcing

St. Joseph's
New Exclusive

PET
SHOP

OPENS SATURDAY
- - AT - -
603 South Eighth

Featuring

LIVE PETS, PET FOODS

ACCESSORIES, REMEDIES, FISH BAIT

In Famous Brands

PET-PAK and MRS. HALFIN'S
BIRD SUPPLIES
GRO-PUP, GAINES and
FRISKIES DOG FOODS

Attractions

- See "Squeaky" the Baby Monkey.
- Polly the Talking Parrot.
- Strange and Colorful tropical fish including fighting Siamese fish and many other birds and animals.
- "FREE" Pet Books and samples.

CARE OF A PET IS AN IMPORTANT PART OF EVERY CHILD'S
TRAINING . . . AND HAPPINESS!

FLINCHPAUGH'S **PET** SHOP

603 South 8th   Phone 4-2988

(Newspaper ad above and News-Press article below)
New Pet Shop to Open Here Tomorrow

*Flinchpaugh"s Pet Shop will open Saturday at 603 south 8th Street. The establishment will feature live pets, pet foods, pet accessories and remedies, as well as fish bait. The shop will have many interesting attractions, which includes **a** baby mon-*

key, talking parrot, and strange, colorful tropical fish. Among the latter will be the fighting fish of Siam. These fish have many strange habits. The males cannot be kept together, as one will kill the other.

Mr. Flinchpaugh was a resident of Kirksville, Mo., several years ago where he operated a wild animal farm. He has been doing this type of work all his life. He invites the public to visit the store and view his complete service for pets. Parents are asked to bring their children. Free pet books and samples are given.

Note: Picture (Below) Margery Flinchpaugh shown in front of the "Flinchpaugh's Pet Shop" at 8th and Messaine.

-1948-

A Safeway grocery store was directly across the street and Ben Magoons was at the other end of the block. On the same side as the pet shop was Croner's drug store on the south corner and Einbenders Department store was south of the drug store. Those Bauer oil jars in the window sell today for hundreds of dollars

Larry Flinchpaugh standing in front of the pet shop
At 8th and Messaine. (603 South Eighth)

My dad's landlord was a dapper looking Jewish man named Abe Goldman. He would come in once a month to collect the rent dressed in a magnificent double breasted suit and sporting silver handled cane.

Larry Flinchpaugh shown above in the
Apple Blossom Parade c. 1949.

133

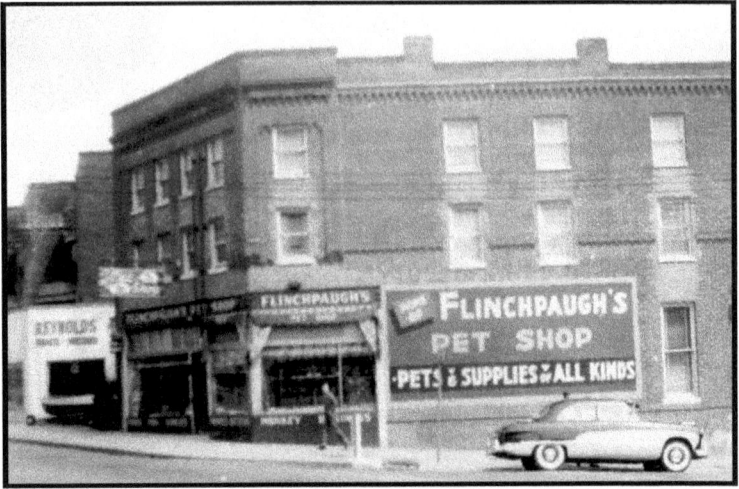

Pet shop at 1202 Frederick Ave –The Red Cross building is directly south and behind the pet shop and Reynolds Boat Shop was two doors East. Al's Market was across the street where. Larry worked for Edna Wisnieswki.

Interior view of the pet shop—Margery and Johnny Flinch-paugh

Interior views of the pet shop at 1202 Frederick

Animal land

The pet shop even had a bird hotel. This was a section by itself and all behind glass. The arrangement made a better display and kept the birds away from drafts. An effect of a cashier's window in the Bird Hotel is created at the left. Birds were a popular item with the buying public. This was not the only bird section in the store. Another one was at the rear where the parrots were kept.

The "Animal Land" photo (previous page) shows the view through the puppy cage and into a monkey cage. The pups are behind glass. Between the two cages is a service way through which caretakers pass to care for the animals.

There was a gas outage in the early 50's in freezing weather that lasted several days. To keep the animals from dying, we temporarily installed a wood heating stove that had to be vented over the front doors transom. Fortunately none of the animals died.

Interior view of the pet shop at 1202 Frederick

This section of the pet shop was called the fish grotto. Bobby Hurst, the son of Mr. And Mrs. William E. Hurst Jr., 2912 South 29th street, is shown here looking at a tank of tropical fish. The tanks are set flush in the wall and are lighted from behind. Tanks, fish and plants to put in them were stocked by the store. The fixtures were built by J. Jack Smith, a St. Joseph contractor.

The pet shop had quite an array of animals for sale. With my dads previous contacts with the circus people and zoos, there was almost no kind of pet that he couldn't locate for his customers.

The longer I worked in the business, the more I came to believe that most people should not have exotic animals for pets. They can be very difficult to care for and as they age

they likely will become temperamental and dangerous-
especially the champanzees.

c. -1953-

Larry Flinchpaugh holding Vicky Lynn

Vicky slept in a baby bassinett for the first few months of
her life. She was cared for by a local pediatrician who
wanted to remain annoyamous. He didn't want to be
known as the "Monkey Doctor." This doctor saved Vicky's
life when at the age of six she almost died of pnemonia.

I guess it would be ok to reveal his name after more than 50 years have passed. It was Doctor Hughes. This wonderful doctor had been my own peditrician and in the 1960's had actually saved my infant son's life also, when he was diagnosed with a twisted colon. My son was rushed to the hospital and before they operated, the barium solution straightened out his colon so the operation was not needed. I believe my son would have died if Dr. Hughes had not made the diagnosis when he did.

Reptile Garden photos at 3727 Frederick

-1956-

Unknown alligator wrestler at the Flinchpaugh Reptile Gardens in St. Joseph, Missouri Note cobra cage behind him. The cobra in that cage is the one that bit Bill White.

Peggy Arnold's South Park Troup 39 visiting the reptile gardens.

Bill White, standing in the snake pit, demonstrating how the fangs work on a rattle snake. Each year many of the local area schools would tour the Reptile Gardens.

Vicky Lynn on right. Note: both have a pacifier in their mouth and Vicky is touching the baby with her foot. I should have taught Vicky sign language to see if she believed in evolution..

141

--"Now its my turn", Vicky says--
Vicky Lynn borrows News-Press photographer, Lewis Shady's camera to take a picture of him.

The python they are displaying was one of the main attractions at the Reptile Gardens. Roy Coy--St.Joseph Museum Director is third from the left, then Johnny Flinchpaugh and Faye Reno at the far right. Note: Airport hanger in back of the Reptile Gardens.(Citizens Bank and Loan is at this location today, 3727 Frederick) Avenue)

142

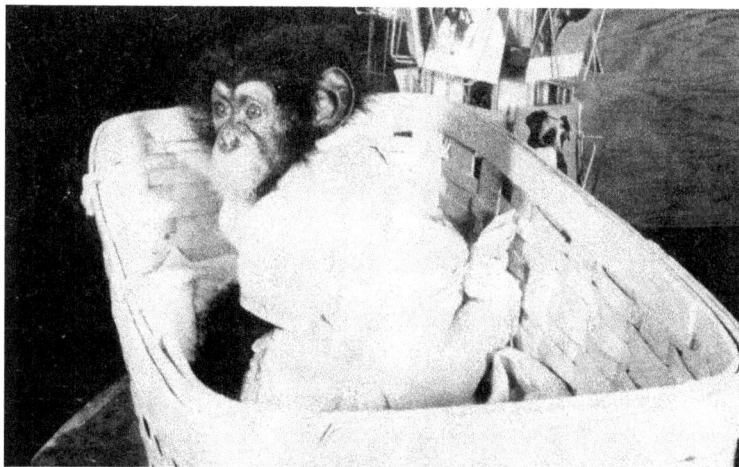

Vicky Lynn--Star of Stage –TV--Screen and Home Movies

Vicky performed at the Krug Park Bowl, was a regular on KFEQ TV and was even featured in a film about primates and evolution. An untold number of our guests at the Reptile Garden took 8mm home movies of Vicky performing her tricks in the late 50's and early 60's.

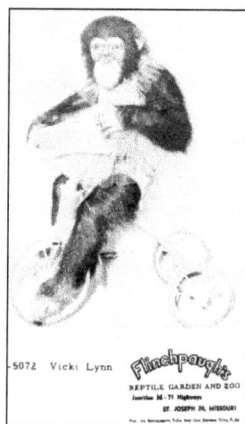

Vicky and Margery Flinchpaugh (left) and Vicky (Right)
(Postcards available to the public c 1957)

143

(Left) Vicky performing at the Krug Park Bowl

Vicky's friend, "Kim", at the Weed Park zoo-Muscatine, Iowa
-1958-

VICKI LYNN and Her
TELEVISION ANIMAL STARS

Trained and
Presented by
J. L. Flinchpaugh

In
Person

See VICKI LYNN exactly as she has appeared in over 120 television shows on coast-to-coast networks. Vicki will do all her tricks, including roller skating, tightwire walking, and many, many more.

VICKY LYNN is the most photographed Chimpanzee in the world today. Here she is shown doing her sensational Hawaiian hula hula dance. (Vicki is insured for $5,000.00.)

Promotional poster for Vicky

Vicky on left—Larry Flinchpaugh (the larger one) on right.)

*School children visiting the reptile gardens in 1955.
Each spring hundred of children would take a field trip to the
reptile gardens.*

*Johnny Flinchpaugh (left) Clyde Reed (Ctr) Fay Reno (right)
This large python was one of the many attractions at the Reptile
Gardens.*

146

Margery, Vicky and Johnny Flinchpaugh

"Hey!, What are you looking at? Can't a girl have some privacy?"

Note: Vicky was more interested in flushing the toilet and watching the water swirl around than learning how to use the toilet.

One of several alligators on display at the reptile gardens.

It was my job to clean out the dead fish that the alligators didn't eat. I would carry a huge club for protection and would always place the clean out 5 gallon waste bucket between me and the alligators to provide a sort of buffer zoan.

One morning one of the alligators got upset for some reason and took a bite out of the bucket. It is a good thing he bit the bucket instead of me because he bit right through the bucket. It looked as if some one had shot four or five holes in the heavy steel bucket as the water poured out.

Billboard advertising Reptile Gardens

148

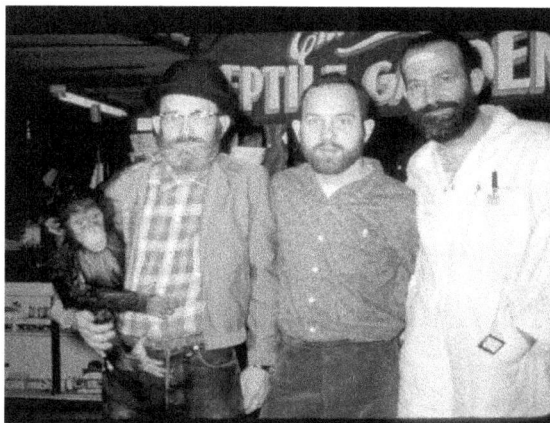

(Left to right) Vicky Lynn Flinchpaugh, Johnny Flinchpaugh, Larry Flinchpaugh and Doctor Deming. Note: Vicky didn't need to grow a beard for the "Centennial."

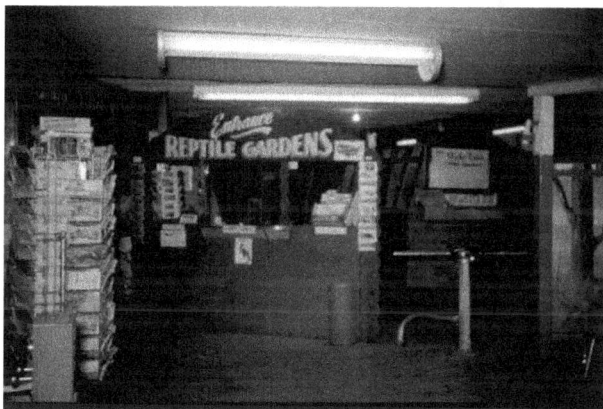

Ticket booth inside of the Reptile Gardens at 3727 Frederick You entered the reptile garden and zoo on the right after purchasing a ticket and the pet shop and gift shop was on the left. To the right of the turn style was a shooting bear machine. If you could hit the bear with a beam of light, he would rare up and turn around and go the opposite direction.

Warning: Don't try this at home!

Once we shipped a large alligator by duct taping him to a large 2x10 wooden plank. We had to use a private carrier as no one else would accept this package with two big menacing eyes stairing at them.

Whoa! Fortunately this was just a photo op. If the elephant had really been trying to enter the building, the entire front of the building would have been destroyed.

This elephant belonged to one of my dad's circus friends. One afternoon the owner asked me to keep his elephant from wandering out on to highway 36 while he used the phone inside. Here I was, all alone with this huge elephant and not having the slightest idea how to stop him if he decided he wanted to cross the highway. I thought well, at least he is big enough the cars would surely see him and stop. Next thing I knew he was heading for the highway. I whistled at him and gave him a command like you would a dog but that didn't work-he kept heading for the highway. Finally I remembered seeing how they did it in the movies. I took the cane I had been given and hooked the end of it on his collar around his neck and gently pulled his head back toward the building. It worked. He slowly moved away from the highway and back towards the building.

Dale Robbins sitting on elephants head holding Vicky

Authors
St. Joe Post Card Collection

Note: Many of these old post cards from the turn of the century did not show an address other than the city. The postman knew everyone by name on his route.

Entrance to Krug Park-St. Joseph, Missouri
This card was mailed in 1912

View in Krug Park-St. Joseph, Missouri
This card was mailed in 1913

153

St. Joseph High School
This card was mailed in 1910

Rubidoux School- St. Joseph, Missouri
Later St. Joseph Junior College
Vicky Lynn took a psychology class here one day.

154

St. Charles Hotel- St. Joseph, Missouri
What a shame this landmark was torn down. I seriously consid-
ered buying the hotel and restoring it to its original glory. As
most projects of this type, the only thing that stopped me was
lack of money. It is a good thing the "Roman Coliseum was not
in St. Joe; there would be a Wal Mart there now or a parking lot.

Court House-St. Joseph, Missouri
Note the horse and buggy at bottom right

155

Missouri Methodist Hospital-St. Joseph, Missouri
Larry Flinchpaugh was born here April 16, 1939 and his son
Mark in 1962

Central Fire Station- St. Joseph, Missouri

Looking West on Felix Street

Lovers Lane—Made famous by Eugene Field
St. Joseph Poet

157

Felix Street
c. 1947
Looking West

Bartlett Trust Building
8th and Frederick
Later "Howett Building"

Patee Market—West Side—Erected 1859
10th between Olive and Lafayette
Photo taken in 1909

This post card was mailed September 22, 1906 to Mr. Ben Ball, Hemple, Missouri from Rushville, Missouri. It only took a one cent stamp to mail.

State Savings Bank at 4th & Felix Street
Organized in 1859 as branch of State Bank of Missouri

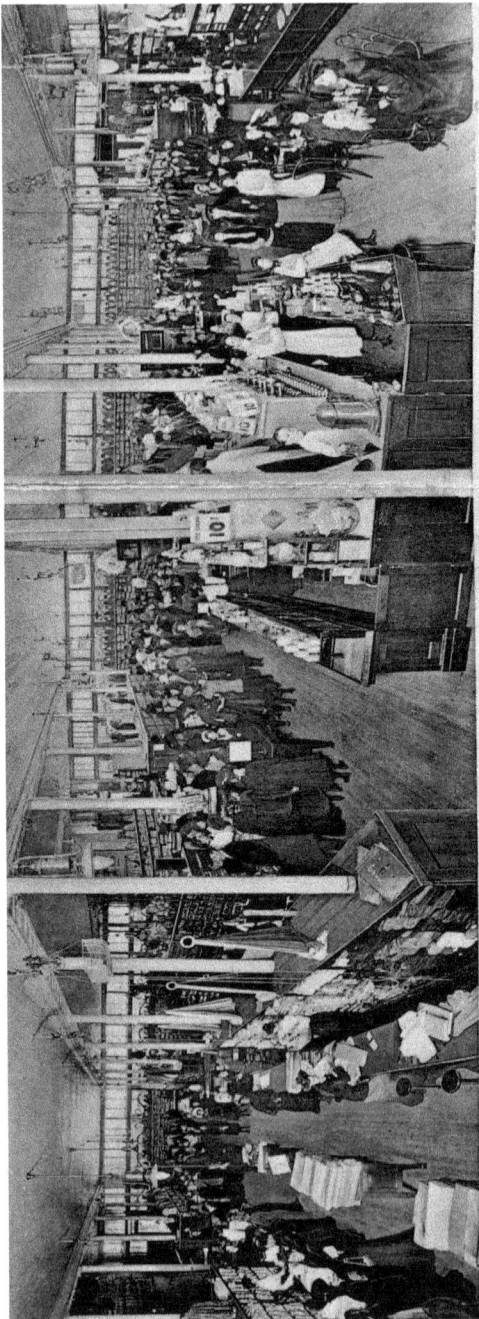

Different Views of The Hirsch Bros. Dry Goods Co., St. Joseph, Mo.

Miscellenous Pictures

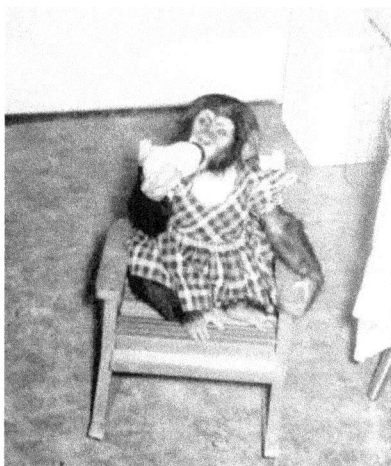

December 27, 1955
Vicky having lunch in Flinchpaugh's
Apartment above the pet shop at 1202
Frederick Ave. St. Joseph, Mo.

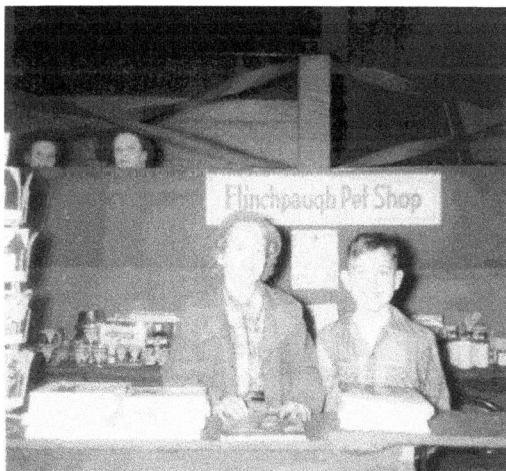

1951 Dog Show at the old auditorium
Larry's mother on left and Larry on right

Clyde Reed and Fay Reno, from the St. Joseph Museum, roping an alligator at Flinchpaugh's Reptile Gardens and Zoo

June 1955

Larry Flinchpaugh's firework stand on the Southwest corner of the Reptile Garden and Zoo parking lot .His sister Jean is shown purchasing fireworks.

162

(Left) 1948 pet shop ad (Right) Back of pet shop business card

163

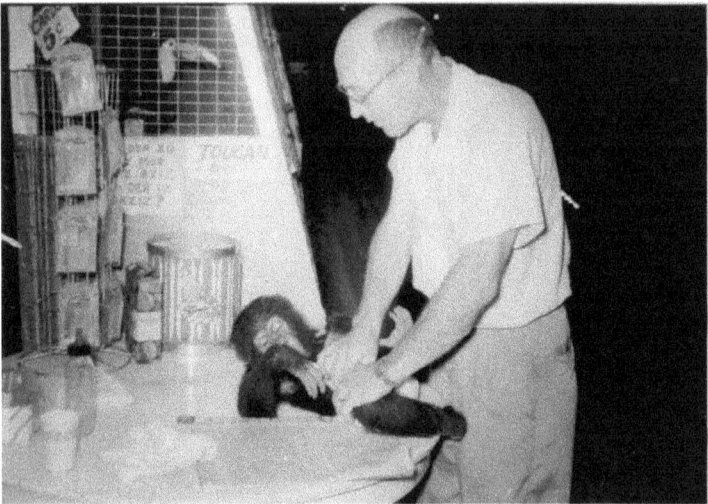

Vicky getting her diaper changed by Johnny Flinchpaugh

Johnny Flinchpaugh holding a bull snake at the Reptile Gardens and Zoo

Vicky Lynn doing her famous hula dance on the left and her "Elvis" impersonation on the right.

Vicky had many friends-Shown here are the famous "Semon" family.

Additional Publications by
J L Flinchpaugh Publishing Company

John Larry Flinchpaugh Autobiography Revised Edition October 2010. One copy each at St., Joseph, Mo Genealogy Library, Kirksville, Mo. City Library and the Cincinnati, Ohio Public Library.

Secrets of Our Hidden Controllers Revealed, November 1, 2009. *Discover how the unelected controllers of our government control our lives and dictate what we do and think.*

Billions For The Bankers-Debts For The People, June 2009. *This 1984 informative 37 page reprint of Sheldon Emry's booklet will give the reader greater insight into our countries monetary system and explains why we must abolish the private Federal Reserve Banking cartel that has, from 1913, been in charge of printing our money and loaning it to the American government with interest. The U.S. Treasury Department can print our money "Interest Free." Forty Eight percent (48%) of our National debt is owed to the private Federal Reserve Bank.*

Growing Up In a Zoo, February 2011 *The story of Larry Flinchpaugh growing up in St. Joseph, Missouri in the 1940's through the 1960's and working in his parents Pet Shop, Zoo, and Reptile Gardens.*

Letters Home From Civil War Soldier Charles W. Gamble to Family--1862-1864 compiled by Mark Flinchpaugh, April 2011.

Movie Documentary *"This Is Our Town, St. Joseph, Missouri"* *Filmed c. 1954*

Vicky was just a common chimpanzee living in the jungles of Africa who came to St. Joseph and became a famous star of movies, stage and television.

www.ingramcontent.com/pod-product-compliance
Lightning Source LLC
Chambersburg PA
CBHW051833090426
42736CB00011B/1775